English for Specific Purposes

Titles in the Resource Books for Teachers series

Beginners
Peter Grundy

Classroom Dynamics
Jill Hadfield

Conversation
Rob Nolasco and Lois Arthur

Creative Poetry Writing
Jane Spiro

Cultural Awareness
Barry Tomalin and Susan Stempleski

Dictionaries
Jon Wright

Drama
Charlyn Wessels

Exam Classes
Peter May

Film
Susan Stempleski and Barry Tomalin

Global Issues
Ricardo Sampedro and Susan Hillyard

Grammar
Scott Thornbury

Grammar Dictation
Ruth Wajnryb

Homework
Lesley Painter

The Internet
Scott Windeatt, David Hardisty,
and D. Eastment

Learner-based Teaching
Colin Campbell and Hanna Kryszewska

Letters
Nicky Burbidge, Peta Gray, Sheila Levy,
and Mario Rinvolucri

Listening
Goodith White

Literature
Alan Duff and Alan Maley

Music and Song
Tim Murphey

Newspapers
Peter Grundy

Project Work 2nd edition
Diana L. Fried-Booth

Pronunciation
Clement Laroy

Role Play
Gillian Porter Ladousse

Storybuilding
Jane Spiro

**Teaching Other Subjects
Through English**
Sheelagh Deller and Chris Price

Teenagers
Gordon Lewis

Vocabulary 2nd edition
John Morgan and Mario Rinvolucri

Writing 2nd edition
Tricia Hedge

Primary Resource Books

Art and Crafts with Children
Andrew Wright

Assessing Young Learners
Sophie Ioannou-Georgiou
and Pavlos Pavlou

Creating Chants and Songs
Carolyn Graham

Creating Stories with Children
Andrew Wright

Drama with Children
Sarah Phillips

Games for Children
Gordon Lewis with Günther Bedson

The Internet and Young Learners
Gordon Lewis

Projects with Young Learners
Diane Phillips, Sarah Burwood,
and Helen Dunford

Storytelling with Children
Andrew Wright

Very Young Learners
Vanessa Reilly and Sheila M. Ward

Writing with Children
Jackie Reilly and Vanessa Reilly

Young Learners
Sarah Phillips

Resource Books for Teachers
series editor Alan Maley

English for Specific Purposes

Keith Harding

OXFORD

UNIVERSITY PRESS

Great Clarendon Street, Oxford OX2 6DP

Oxford University Press is a department of the University of Oxford.
It furthers the University's objective of excellence in research, scholarship,
and education by publishing worldwide in

Oxford New York

Auckland Cape Town Dar es Salaam Hong Kong Karachi
Kuala Lumpur Madrid Melbourne Mexico City Nairobi
New Delhi Shanghai Taipei Toronto

With offices in

Argentina Austria Brazil Chile Czech Republic France Greece
Guatemala Hungary Italy Japan Poland Portugal Singapore
South Korea Switzerland Thailand Turkey Ukraine Vietnam

OXFORD and OXFORD ENGLISH are registered trade marks of
Oxford University Press in the UK and in certain other countries

ISBN-13: 987 019 442575 9
ISBN-10: 0 19 442575 9

Printed in Spain by Unigraf S.L.

Acknowledgements

The authors and publisher are grateful to those who have given permission to reproduce the following extracts and adaptations of copyright material:

Skills for Life: Materials for Embedded Learning, Trowel occupations: example of construction company organogram; sample programme of work for the building trade; safety instructions for herbicide Based on DFES Skills for Life Materials for Embedded Learning: Horticulture. Crown Copyright 2006, published by the Department for Education and Skills. Reproduced under terms of the Click-Use licence.

British National Corpus – Variations in English Words and Phrases www.natcorp.ox.ac.uk. Reproduced by kind permission.

Extracts from *International Express* by Liz Taylor and Keith Harding © Oxford University Press 2005 and extract from *Going International* by Keith Harding © Oxford University Press 1998, reproduced by permission from Oxford University Press.

'Zap! Go to the top of the class' by Tania Branigan, copyright Guardian News and Media Limited 2001.

Specification of British Airways Fleet reproduced by kind permission of British Airways Press Office.

Illustrations by: Stefan Chabluk pp. 4, 84,102; Martin Cottam p. 94; Dylan Gibson pp. 127, 147; Ann Johns p. 77.

Safety notices on pages 142 and 147 by kind permission of Signs and Labels Limited.

Contents

5 Using numbers and figures

Activity	Level	Time (minutes)	Aims	

The author and series editor

Keith Harding was born in London and educated at St Albans School and at King's College, Cambridge. He completed a PhD in History at the University of Sussex in 1983, before beginning his career in EFL.

He worked in language schools in Brighton and International House, London, before joining St Giles International where he has worked as a teacher, teacher trainer (CELTA), Director of Studies, and, since 1994, as Principal. He has worked at both the London Highgate and San Francisco centres. He completed his RSA Diploma in 1985, and has taught all levels and aspects of EFL.

For Oxford University Press he has written *Going International* (1998), and co-authored *High Season* (1994) and *International Express Intermediate* (New edition, 2005). He is currently involved in the Oxford English for Careers series.

Alan Maley worked for The British Council from 1962 to 1988, serving as English Language Officer in Yugoslavia, Ghana, Italy, France, and China, and as Regional Representative in South India (Madras). From 1988 to 1993 he was Director-General of the Bell Educational Trust, Cambridge. From 1993 to 1998 he was Senior Fellow in the Department of English Language and Literature of the National University of Singapore, and from 1998 to 2002 he was Director of the graduate programme at Assumption University, Bangkok. He is currently a freelance consultant and Visiting Professor at Leeds Metropolitan University. Among his publications are *Literature*, in this series, *Beyond Words*, *Sounds Interesting*, *Sounds Intriguing*, *Words*, *Variations on a Theme*, and *Drama Techniques in Language Learning* (all with Alan Duff), *The Mind's Eye* (with Françoise Grellet and Alan Duff), *Learning to Listen* and *Poem into Poem* (with Sandra Moulding), *Short and Sweet*, and *The English Teacher's Voice*.

Foreword

English for Specific Purposes (ESP) first came to prominence in the 1970s. It came about largely in response to increasing numbers of overseas students coming to pursue university studies in the UK and other metropolitan countries, and to the setting up of new universities in the Persian Gulf, Saudi Arabia, Iran, Malaysia, and elsewhere. In both cases there was a call for courses to meet the immediate needs of students to enable them to pursue their subject studies in English.

Since then ESP has lost some of its early lustre, and has seen the hiving off of English for Business and English for Academic Purposes as largely independent focuses. Nonetheless there has been a steady demand for courses related to the immediate needs of students rather than to the ENOP (English for No Obvious Purposes) offered in most secondary education institutions.

Why then the need for the present book? A number of inter-connected trends suggest that ESP is again emerging as a key strand in the ELT context. As English gathers momentum as the main language of international communication, it is perceived as the language of career opportunity, so the pressure grows for teaching to be more directly employment-related. In parallel with this, the output from secondary schools is tending to be at higher levels of proficiency, so a re-hash of the general English courses at later stages of learning becomes less acceptable. Furthermore, the rapid growth of 'Content and Language Integrated Learning'—reflected in the recent book in this series *Teaching Other Subjects Through English*—means that content-based instruction is filtering downwards into the secondary system itself. All of this adds up to a need for materials directly related to vocational and professional purposes.

In this book the author offers a coherent response to the very diverse learning situations and learners typically encountered in ESP contexts. He offers 15 different focal areas, ranging from Catering to Law, from Medicine to Retail and sales. He has succeeded in finding commonalities across the wide variety of ESP areas, for example the need to focus on specialist vocabulary, the use of visual and numerical displays and the need to use equipment efficiently and safely.

The book will be of great value to teachers who need to relate their teaching of English directly to the vocational and professional needs of their students.

Alan Maley

Introduction

'What exactly do you do?'

Soon after I gained my initial teaching qualification, I was given a job teaching English at the Soviet Trade Delegation in north London. This was in the early 1980s. I arrived at the Delegation keen and excited, equipped with a 'Present. Practise. Produce.' approach, ideas about communicative language teaching, my 'ten stages for doing a listening', and so on, plus a few current General English coursebooks.

I entered the room to be met with a group of eight burly be-suited Russian gentlemen. They didn't look a bit like my friendly multi-national Teaching Practice group. Nevertheless, I plunged into it with a 'getting to know you' activity. My eight gentlemen refused to stand up and mingle, so we went round the class instead: 'Hi, I'm Keith and I'm a teacher from London. Tell me about your partner.' They ignored my instruction and instead introduced themselves: 'My name is Mr Lubichkin, I am economic adviser.' 'My name is Mr Demidov, I am economic adviser.' And so on. I responded weakly to one or two: 'Oh, that's interesting, and what *exactly* do you do?' Response: 'I am economic adviser.'

Somehow I got through that first lesson, but I realised how poorly prepared I was for what was in effect my first ESP lesson. No needs analysis, no appropriately selected materials, no awareness of who my students really were. These days most initial training courses include some work on ESP, but I suspect that many newly-qualified teachers find themselves in situations not too dissimilar from my Soviet nightmare—and many newly-qualified teachers do indeed have to teach ESP early on in their careers. This book aims to provide activities that will help not only the newly-qualified teacher in the ESP classroom, but also the more experienced teacher looking for fresh ideas.

As a postscript to this story, many years later, after the fall of Communism, I read that the Soviet Trade Delegation had been bugged by British intelligence throughout the 1980s. I like to think that somewhere in the basement of MI5 is a tape with my trembling voice on it, saying: 'Oh, that's very interesting—what exactly does an economic adviser do?' Interrogation techniques, I suspect, as well as ESP methodology, have moved on since then.

What is ESP?

Whereas 'General English' is sometimes, perhaps unfairly, labelled English for No Obvious Purpose, in ESP—English for Specific Purposes—the purpose for learning the language is paramount and relates directly to what the learner needs to do in their vocation or job. One definition states that 'ESP is designed to meet specific needs of the learner', it 'makes use of the underlying methodology and activities of the discipline it serves', and it 'is centred on the language (grammar, lexis, register), skills, discourse and genres appropriate to these activities.' (Dudley-Evans and St John. 1998. *Developments in ESP*, CUP). Perhaps a simpler definition is that ESP teaches 'the language for getting things done'.

In all definitions of ESP two elements are axiomatic: the sense of purpose and the sense of vocation. In ESP the practical application and use of language overrides other aspects of language learning. The vocation can be anything from A to Z, from architects to zoologists, by way of bricklayers, lawyers, and tour guides. The sense of purpose gives the language work an immediacy and a relevance which is perhaps not always found in other sectors of ELT, particularly of the 'General English' variety, and can present the teacher with challenges; but it also makes ESP an interesting and exciting area for teachers.

In an industry that loves its acronyms, ESP has spawned more than most: EAP, EBP, EMP, EOP, EPP, EST, EVP* to name just a few. We will only use the term 'ESP' in this book. ESP is a comprehensive term and it includes English for Business and English for Academic purposes, but as these are such developed and well-established areas of ELT in their own right, we have not put them to the forefront here— although there will be significant reference to these fields and many of the activities will have application to students of English for Business and English for Academic Purposes. In this book we are looking at the world of work in general and the main focus for the activities presented here will be the vocational learner, in the widest sense, and including learners in the professions, industry, and technology.

* *English for Academic Purposes, English for Business Purposes, English for Medical Purposes, English for Occupational Purposes, English for Professional Purposes, English for Science and Technology, English for Vocational Purposes.*

How important is ESP?

ESP has been growing in importance for many years now. There are a number of factors behind this:
- The increase in vocational learning and training throughout the world, as education becomes less academic and esoteric, and more practical and application-oriented. Students want their studies to

lead to something useful. Economies and markets want to employ people with vocational skills.

- Globalization continues to spread, and globalization has clearly chosen English as its language of communication. In a shrinking world, English as the language of international communication is spreading faster and faster. It is also spreading downwards and outwards to people who'd never needed English before. It's not just the politician, the business leader, and the academic professor who need to speak to international colleagues and clients: it's also the hotel receptionist, the nurse, and the site foreman. And new groups constantly appear—call centre operatives, construction workers moving within the European Union are two such recent examples.
- At the same time, General English is being taught throughout the world at earlier ages with increasing success. As this trend continues, students will leave their primary education having already covered the traditional 'General English' syllabus, and, regardless of how competent they have become, they will not wish to repeat the same old merry-go-round at secondary and tertiary level—their English studies need an application, a purpose.

The emphasis, since the mid 1980s, on English as an International Language (EIL) (through the work of Jennifer Jenkins and others), on the internationalization of the structures and usage of English and on the growth in the need for intercultural awareness, also owes a lot to these factors. In many ways, ESP is the coal-face of International English: it is its practical application. And it's not just the coal-face: it's the production line, the operating theatre, the reception desk, and the building site.

Although English for Business and English for Academic Purposes have become established as the pillars of ELT beyond 'General English', the wider definition of ESP as looking at the world of work in general has perhaps been neglected, with a lack of training for newly-qualified teachers and with support materials hard to find, limited, and often too sector-specific. This book hopes to redress this and to recognize the broader approach to ESP—the world of work in general—as the crucial component of what might be termed 'applied ELT'.

What is the role of the ESP teacher?

It has been argued that the ESP practitioner has 'five key roles':
- Teacher or language consultant
- Course designer and materials provider
- Researcher—not just gathering material, but also understanding the nature of the material of the ESP specialism
- Collaborator—working with subject teachers and subject teaching
- Evaluator—constantly evaluating the materials and the course design, as well as setting assessment tests and achievement tests.

Activities in this book will provide material for all of these roles.

Does the ESP teacher need to be an expert in the vocational area their students work in? The simple answer is: You don't need to be an expert, but you need to have some understanding of the subject area. Scrivener (*Learning Teaching*, Macmillan 2005) reassures the worried teacher when faced with teaching an ESP course for nuclear engineers that: 'You know about English; they know about the topic. Put the two together, and you have the potential for some exciting lessons.' He goes on to say that what ESP really means is: 'Go on teaching all the normal English you already teach in all the ways you know how to do already, but use lexis, examples, topics and contexts that are, as far as possible, relevant to the students and practise relevant specific skills.'

However, there's probably a bit more to it than Scrivener implies. Certainly the teacher will need—as a minimum—to understand what is involved in the specific area, and will need to be aware of the language requirements involved. Beyond this it will help if they can relate to the mindset and spirit (the 'soul', if you like) of the special area or vocation. Different professions and vocations have different ways of thinking, different cultures, and this is reflected in the way they need and use the English language. Understanding these ways and cultures will enable the teacher to teach more effectively. There are stories of ELT teachers on courses for bricklayers becoming bricklayers themselves. That must be the ultimate sign of a successful course—the transfusion of knowledge and mutual expertise.

What are the characteristics of the ESP learner?

The diverse range of subjects and vocations covered by ESP will always make generalizations difficult. Nevertheless, there are some consistencies and tendencies that ESP teachers will often meet in their learners. It is probably useful to divide ESP learners into two broad categories. Firstly, there are those already working in their specialism or at an advanced stage of their training. Secondly, there are those who are pre-work and who will probably be younger (for example, 16–18), and where it can not be expected that they have much detailed knowledge of their specialism. The following characteristics apply mainly to the former category.

- The ESP learner has a further purpose. He or she is learning English in order to achieve something specific beyond the language itself.
- The further purpose of the ESP learner will usually involve skills that are very different from the skills involved in learning a language. These skills will often be practical and manual, but not always.

- The ESP learner has often not succeeded as a language learner in the past—after all, they have chosen to pursue a vocation and a purpose that is not language-based.
- The ESP learner will probably be studying English at the same time as studying their subject or doing a full-time job (neither of which is likely to be language-based). He or she may well come to the ESP class tired and distracted.
- The ESP learner may be there reluctantly, perhaps because their line manager has told them to be there.
- ESP learners in the same class are unlikely to have the same, or even a similar, level of English. The teacher must expect mixed levels and will need to have strategies and activities to allow for differentiation.
- But against this must be set the fact that the students will usually be studying in the same ESP area. It is rare to have a class containing lawyers, nurses, and bricklayers at the same time; but it is possible to have varied classes within a specialism—for example, doctors, nurses, radiologists, and administrators.

The second (pre-work) category of ESP learners will demonstrate many of the same characteristics, but they will represent an even greater challenge to the teacher in that they have not yet developed knowledge or possibly even interest in their specialism. Motivation will be a key need—not just in English language studies, but in the specialism itself. Developing the two motivations in tandem is however an exciting prospect for the teacher and links in with recent ELT concepts of CLIL (Content and Language Integrated Learning) covered in *Teaching Other Subjects Through English* (OUP Resource Book for Teachers series).

What do ESP specialisms have in common?

It might be thought that, by definition, specialisms in ESP will not have much in common with each other. For example, what could a doctor, a plumber, a motor mechanic, and a meteorologist have in common when it comes to language needs?

Well, for a start they all have specific needs which the teacher will need to identify and build into the course. They all have to understand technical specialized vocabulary and documentation, and often use graphical, diagrammatic, and number-based information sources. They all have an identifiable working environment; they all use equipment and will need to train or be trained in its use, and will therefore need to know how to describe it and its purpose. They all have to interact with the public in some way, and operate within health and safety and other legal constraints. They will all need to reflect on and evaluate their own performance, and work with other team members. Beyond that, there is also the fact that these four particular ESP learners will all deal with circulatory systems at some point in their work: the circulation of blood through the human body, the pumping of water through a cooling system, the circulation of petrol through a car engine, and the cycle of rainfall in weather systems.

These common areas form the basis of the chapter titles: needs analysis and course design; organizational structures; vocabulary; processes, procedures, and operating systems; using numbers and figures; customer care and quality assurance; health and safety; evaluation and review. Preparing for the world of work is thus the organizing idea behind this resource book, and the activities aim to cross the sectional boundaries between different specialisms. Having established the fact that there can be common approaches in ESP teaching, however, it is important to also be aware of the differences—different needs, different learning styles, and different genres of texts and interaction. Genre—the particular style and features of text or discourse related to the specialism—and genre analysis are an important part of ESP, and will feature in several of the activities.

What general approaches will the ESP teacher need to take?

The ESP teacher will need to take an approach that meets the particular needs of the ESP learner. This will involve emphasizing certain areas of mainstream ELT practice, rather than inventing wholly new ones. It will certainly mean interacting closely with the students and their needs. But the General English or newly-trained teacher should be reassured that key concepts such as being communicative, using authentic materials, analyzing language in a practical way, and generally relating to the students on as many levels as possible, are just as true in ESP as in General English—if not more so.

There are some general do's and don'ts:
- Think about what is needed. Don't just blindly follow a grammar syllabus (or functional syllabus, or topical syllabus) that is simply taken 'off the peg'.
- Understand the nature of your students' subject area or vocation. Talk to them about their job or vocation. Be interested: ask to visit the facility, lab, factory, workplace. And if they are pre-work, get them thinking about where they might eventually be using their English—in other words, give them a vision of their future.
- Spend time working out their language needs in relation to the subject.
- Use contexts, texts, and situations from the students' subject area. Whether they are real or simulated, they will naturally involve the language the students need.

- Exploit authentic material that the students use in their specialism or vocation—and don't be put off by the fact that it may not look like 'normal' English.
- Make the tasks authentic as well as the texts. Get the students doing things with the material that they actually need to do in their work.
- Motivate the students with variety, relevance, and fun. Remember that they may be tired and that they may not share your own love of the language.
- Above all, try to take the classroom into the real world that the students inhabit, and bring their real world into the classroom.

How can activities be transferred across the sectors?

We have already argued that the different ESP specialisms have a lot in common. In this book we are taking an approach that stresses the common core and transferable nature of ESP specialisms, and the teacher will need to emphasize this to the learners so that they are not met with the reaction: 'What has this got to do with my job?' Looking at one's position from outside and seeing it in a wider context is always healthy, but the learner may need help in appreciating this. Suggestions will be made in all the activities as to how they can be transferred to other specialisms—for example, in Chapter 1 when looking at the text types and documentation used in a particular specialism and identifying the sub-skills involved in reading such texts, and in Chapter 3 when looking at the most important items of equipment for a 'box of tricks' for different vocations.

In addition, some key steps can be followed by the teacher:
- Clearly explain the objectives.
- Explain that even if a document or activity isn't from the students' own field it contains structures, vocabulary (often sub-technical or enabling), and language approaches that can be transferred to their field and used in a similar way.
- In any document or material highlight the terms and language that can be transferred.
- Always ensure that there is a 'transfer' stage to the activity, when the content is related directly to their work situation (as will be suggested in our activities).

Is ESP a matter of life and death?

We started this introduction with a personal anecdote, so let's finish it with another. Many years ago I found myself in a London hospital with a very nasty and bloody wound to my left eye (the result of a cricket match that went horribly wrong, but that is another story).

Lying in the treatment room with blood pouring down my face, I found I had a Spanish-speaking doctor and a Chinese-speaking nurse. While their professional skills were not in doubt, neither of them spoke good English and neither of them could understand each other very well. Over the ensuing twenty or thirty minutes I found myself explaining where the doctor wanted the injection for the local anaesthetic to be made, providing the words 'scissors' and 'thread', and clarifying the length of thread needed. An ESP course including work on the language of prepositions of place and location, the lexis of basic medical equipment, and the language of lengths and dimensions would certainly have been of value. It might also have reduced my anxiety and minimized my pain.

This was not a matter of life or death, but there could have been similar situations where the stakes were much higher. Teachers of ESP do an extremely important job!

How is this book organized?

The activities in this book are arranged into chapters which are intended to reflect the shared concepts behind ESP teaching, whatever the specialism. As far as possible, the activities are transferable—in other words they can be used across the range of specialisms, albeit often with some adaptation.

Chapter 1, 'Needs analysis and course design', aims to help the teacher to uncover the mindset and culture of the specialism they are working with, and to find its key features. It looks at activities to help with needs analysis and course design, both of which are essential in ESP teaching, and, related to this, how authentic materials can be gathered and exploited.

Chapter 2, 'Organizational structures', looks at the detail of how the mindset and culture operate in practice, with activities that exploit the whole area of organizational structures, job descriptions, and instructions and briefings.

Chapter 3, 'Vocabulary', presents activities to develop the learning and use of lexis related to the specialism—either technical or sub-technical. Such vocabulary is an obvious but vital component of an ESP course.

Chapter 4, 'Processes, procedures, and operating systems', focuses on the stages and processes involved in the specialism, and some of the core generic language that is used. Many of the activities are concerned with mechanical relations and systems. It is not, however, simply about machines and technology: the service sector and the professions, for example, have systems that have similarities to mechanical and technological operations.

Chapter 5, 'Using numbers and figures', explores the different ways in which graphical, diagrammatic, and number-based information operates both receptively and productively in a wide range of ESP specialisms. This 'cross-curricular' dimension is a fundamental feature of ESP.

Chapter 6, 'Customer care and quality assurance', primarily looks at activities related to the service and professional sectors where dealing with customers and clients is of paramount importance. But again the issues can often be relevant to all sectors.

Chapter 7, 'Health and safety', explores an area of growing importance across all sectors. Activities are presented around the common area of looking after yourself, your colleagues, and your customers in a working environment.

Chapter 8, 'Evaluation and review', presents activities aimed at self-evaluation, self-improvement, both in terms of the learner's vocation or job and in terms of development on the English language course.

How is each activity organized?

ESP covers a vast range of vocational and professional areas. The main specialisms covered in this book are:
- Administration and office work
- Architecture and design
- Business and commerce
- Catering and food production
- Construction and building trades
- Engineering
- Horticulture and agriculture
- Information technology
- Law
- Marketing and advertising
- Mechanical and motor trades
- Medicine and health care
- Phone-based services
- Retail and sales
- Tourism and travel

Many of the activities in the book are classified 'General', meaning that they are of relevance to all specialisms and that any examples used are not specific to any particular vocation or profession. Other activities use an example from one area and then suggest parallel examples for other areas.

Each activity is organized under the following headings:

Level

This may vary according to the adaptations you can make. Usually it indicates the minimum level that the activity is recommended for, although this will vary in different contexts, and of course you know your students best.

Time

The time given is a suggestion for guidance and may vary with different classes. Sometimes suggestions are made for splitting up longer activities over two or more lessons.

Aims

These are headed 'Language' and 'Other'.

Language

The activity may require knowledge of—or give the opportunity to explore—specific grammatical language. This may be useful if you are relating your course to a grammar-based or a General English syllabus. This heading is omitted when no specific language points are practised.

Other

This signposts the skills the students will need to carry out the activity. The aims of an activity may be related to language points or developing language skills. They may also relate to wider areas, such as exploring genres, improving learning skills, discussing and developing working concepts and practices.

Example specialism

Although all the activities are designed to have as wide an application as possible, many will often be based on material and texts relating to a specific specialism. Where this is not the case, this sub-heading will simply be 'General'.

Transfer

This section will indicate specialisms where the activity may be of particular relevance, and also any other points that are important when transferring the activity to another field. This heading may be omitted when the Example specialism is 'General'.

Materials

Anything you need to have available in order to do the activity. This could be photocopies, worksheets, or documents, or it could be realia based on the specialism that you are teaching. It is a good idea to have a 'box of tricks' of such items related to the ESP sector you are involved with, and to always have it available for use.

Preparation

Anything you need to do before the lesson begins.

Procedure

This shows, in clear numbered steps, how to set up and carry out the activity.

Variation

These include ideas on how to adapt the activity to suit different levels, alternative topics, or other ways of delivering the activity.

Follow-up

Where appropriate, optional extra activities are suggested which give the learner the opportunity to take the activity beyond the classroom.

Comments

These are additional notes and advice that will help you to use the activity appropriately.

These headings are designed to provide a familiar and user-friendly template for the teacher. You might find that you have ideas of your own, maybe activities that you have used successfully in the past. If you do, and if you want to share them, we have provided a template on the OUP Resource Books for teachers website http://www.oup.com/elt/teacher/rbt. You are welcome to send your ideas in, using the template, for possible publication on the website.

1
Needs analysis and course design

Finding out about and analyzing the needs of the students is vital in ESP teaching. In fact one of the main contributions of ESP to the wider world of English Language Teaching has been the development of thorough needs analysis. This chapter provides some activities to help discover these needs and thus to translate them into course design.

Before starting out, however, you will need to know as much as possible about the learning situation of the students. In particular:

- Is it an intensive course (concentrated into one period of time) or an extensive course (spread out over a longer period of time)?
- Is it assessed or non-assessed?
- Is it meeting immediate needs (learners are working and studying in parallel) or delayed needs (students are pre-experience and will be working on the specialism sometime in the future)?
- Is the group homogenous or heterogenous? For example, are they all at the same level of English? Do they all have the same level of knowledge of, and involvement in, the specialism?
- Is the course designed by the teacher or the institution or negotiated with the learner?

If the answer to the last question is that the course is designed by the institution and a strict external syllabus has to be followed, that does not negate the need for your own needs analysis and for some of the activities suggested—hopefully, the two will coalesce, but if they don't you may need to bring it to the attention of the institution.

Once you have got these points clear, you can start to work on the particular needs of your ESP students. Bear in mind that needs analysis is not just an initial one-off activity—it should be an ongoing process, and the activities in this chapter can be used at different stages in the course. First and foremost, you will need to think about how much you know about the specialism. 1.1, 'Knowing the subject', suggests a way in which you can test your knowledge by involving the students and then go on to build a needs analysis together. 1.2, 'What do you need' to 1.5, 'What do you need to read', offer a variety of ways of approaching needs analysis. 1.6, 'The authentic materials bank' suggests ways of gathering authentic material, and together with 1.5 relates to the important ESP area of genre-analysis.

By definition the needs analysis activities so far described will be identifying the particular features and culture of the specialism. 1.7,

'The A to Z of job skills' to 1.9, 'The classroom as workplace' focus on this more directly, and seek to define the culture often in relation to other specialisms. All these activities lead automatically to course design, but 1.10, 'Identifying target events' looks at this in more detail.

1.1 Knowing the subject

Level All levels

Time 20–40 minutes

Aims To familiarize yourself with the subject of the specialism of your students at the start of a course, so as to more easily identify their needs; to show the students that you are interested in and knowledgeable about their subject.

Sample topic General

Materials Photocopies of fact-sheet—one per student.

Preparation

The preparation is in fact the main part of this activity, as the idea is for you (the teacher) to find out as much as you can about the specialism of the students you are going to be teaching.

1 Research, using whatever sources you think appropriate (the Internet, books, your own knowledge, local careers departments, colleagues in other departments, etc.—as well as any profiles you may have for the students you are teaching), and answer these questions:
   • What does the job/specialism involve?
   • What subjects do the students usually study at school?
   • What qualifications are there in the specialism, and how long does the training usually take?
   • What different jobs are covered by the specialism?
   • What is the workplace like?
   • What possible career paths are there?
   • In what situations will English be used?
   • What language skills—such as reading, writing, listening, or speaking—will be most used?
   • What materials and resources are used?

2 Use the information you find to prepare a fact-sheet about the specialism. Do not worry if you are not sure about some of the information, as the aim is for the students to put you right. In fact it is a good idea to include one or two deliberate mistakes or any myths about the specialism (although not too many, as this may undermine your credibility!).

Procedure

1 Explain to the class that you have prepared a fact-sheet about their specialism, but that you are not sure if it is completely correct.

2   Give out the fact-sheet and get the students in pairs to read it through, check it for accuracy, correct if necessary, and add any more information that they think is appropriate.

3   Get the students to re-group in different pairs and compare their revisions.

4   Feedback to the whole class. Make sure you show genuine interest in the details of their specialism and its related subjects.

Variation

If you do not want to spend so much time researching details, get the students themselves to write down the facts. They could do this by answering the questions listed under 'Preparation'. For added interest, get them to each write one fact and pass the paper to the left for the fact to be checked or corrected and another fact added, then continue passing round.

Follow-up

Move on to a more conventional needs analysis (for example, 1.2, 'What do you need?'), which they will now approach having thought about the features of their specialism in some detail.

1.2 What do you need?

Level	Elementary to advanced
Time	45 minutes, with a second session of 20 minutes (this can be done as homework)
Aims	To discover the students' needs for the course and to involve them in the creation of their own needs analysis.
Sample topic	Business and commerce
Transfer	Activity can be transferred to any specialism. You may need to adjust the balance between topic, function, and skill.
Materials	Contents page of a standard General English coursebook; photocopies of Worksheet 1.2, 'Needs analysis'—one per student.

Preparation

1   Think about the best format that a 'Needs analysis' for your group should take. Try to replicate the type of information formats that they will meet in their work. For example, if they work in business and have to make presentations, consider using a Powerpoint presentation at step 5.

2   Prepare a model 'Needs analysis'—but be ready to adapt it. A model for Business English students is provided.

Procedure

1 Give out the contents page (or 'map') of a standard General English coursebook.

2 Focus attention on the topic, function, and skills part of the contents map. They may use different labels (for example, topic may be under 'vocabulary'). Avoid looking at 'grammar', as this may distract from the aims of the activity.

3 Ask the students to decide if any of the items in the General English contents page are relevant to their ESP studies.

4 In groups, brainstorm items that they feel they will need to cover in the course under the headings: 'Topic', 'Functions', 'Skills'.

5 The groups then present their ideas to the rest of the class, preferably in a relevant format.

6 Consolidate the students' lists with any ideas of your own and produce a 'Needs analysis' master list. (This may need to be done for a second day.)

7 Get the students to individually complete the 'Needs analysis', scoring each item from 1–5 depending on how important they think it is for them.

Worksheet 1.2

Needs analysis

Please take time to complete this form and send it back to us before you start your course. It will help us to customize your course and to meet your specific needs.

Name: _____

Nationality: _____

Occupation: _____

Rate each item 1–5. Most important for you = 5; least important for you = 1.

Which Business English **topics** would you like to study?

☐ Business news/Market trends

☐ Management

☐ Marketing/Advertising

☐ Sales

☐ Business English for social purposes

☐ Company structures

☐ Information Technology

☐ Law

☐ Trade

☐ Globalization

☐ Leadership

☐ Recruitment and Human Resources

☐ Banking and finance

☐ Ethics in business

☐ Economic policies

☐ Production

☐ Cross-cultural awareness

☐ Time management

☐ Setting goals

Which of the following **functions** do you need to practise in English?

- [ ] Telephone English
- [ ] Meetings
- [ ] Negotiations
- [ ] Presentations
- [ ] Interviewing
- [ ] Decision-making
- [ ] Arranging schedules and appointments, making travel arrangements
- [ ] Describing processes
- [ ] Making suggestions

- [ ] Introductions, small talk, welcoming a visitor
- [ ] Offering praise, complaints
- [ ] Asking permission
- [ ] Asking for advice
- [ ] Agreeing/disagreeing, persuading, clarifying, and interrupting
- [ ] Summarizing
- [ ] Obtaining information

Which Business English **skills** would you like to improve?

Speaking

- [ ] Public speaking
- [ ] Describing things when you don't know the exact word
- [ ] Staying on a topic
- [ ] Persuasive questioning
- [ ] Dealing with communication problems

Reading

- [ ] Reports
- [ ] Correspondence
- [ ] Articles, journals, abstracts, and trade publications
- [ ] Quick reading for specific information and key points

Writing

- [ ] Reports
- [ ] Taking notes on talks
- [ ] Memos/messages
- [ ] Emails
- [ ] Business letters
- [ ] Cover letters and CVs
- [ ] Forms: applications, proposals, and invoices

Listening

- [ ] To radio, TV, and Internet broadcasts
- [ ] For the main idea/key points
- [ ] To natural speech
- [ ] To people from non-English-speaking countries

Photocopiable © Oxford University Press

Variation

Get individual groups to take just one of the head words—'Topic', 'Function', or 'Skills'—and then explain to others and invite additions.

Follow-up

Use the information you have discovered, including the scores for level of importance, to design your course.

The functional aspect of the activity leads into 1.3, 'Function cards'.

1.3 Function cards

Level Elementary to advanced

Time 20–30 minutes

Aims LANGUAGE Functional language in general.

OTHER To identify the functional language that students need in their specialism; to diagnose level of language needs.

Sample topic Mechanical and motor trades

Transfer Activity can be transferred to any specialism.

Materials Photocopies of Function cards—one set per group.

Preparation

Prepare a series of function cards. Write a different function on a piece of paper or card. A list of functions is provided on the next page and you can add and delete according to what you think will be involved in the specialism you are teaching, but make sure you include some that might not be obviously used in the specialism. Make as many sets as you need in order to work with three or four students per group.

Procedure

1 Explain and demonstrate the rules of the game:
   • Students take turns to take a card from the top of the pile, they have to say whether the function is used in their specialism or not.
   • If yes, they have to provide a situation when it is used.

Example for motor mechanics *Giving instructions—Telling an assistant how to change a wheel.*

   • For a bonus point they can provide a model example (*First you have to remove the nuts*). This can be thrown open to the rest of the group. Remember the function can be written or spoken.

2 Divide the class into teams of three or four. Appoint one person in each group to be the scorer. You will have to be the judge of the model examples, so be ready to be called over. When judging the model examples, make notes of student errors. This will help you to diagnose the level of student competence and help you to accurately pitch future lessons.

3 Play the game. Students should keep the cards that have functions that are used in their specialism. You will need to collect these so that you can incorporate them into your course plan.

Greeting a colleague	Introducing yourself	Introducing a colleague	Asking for information
Giving information	Giving instructions	Giving orders	Giving advice
Asking for help and advice	Explaining rules	Explaining where something is	Explaining a process or procedure
Making a suggestion	Putting forward a formal proposal	Asking for clarification	Interrupting
Inviting someone to do something	Making an offer	Congratulating	Apologizing
	Dealing with a complaint	Describing a piece of equipment or machinery	

Photocopiable © Oxford University Press

Follow-up

Integrate the identified functions into the syllabus and course plan. Use the errors you gathered to pitch the correct level and work on appropriate language areas.

Comments

The game can still be played even if you have only a small number of students, or even on a one-to-one basis.

1.4 What do you wear? What do you use?

Level Elementary to intermediate

Time 30 minutes

Aims LANGUAGE Language of purpose (*in order to, because, it's used for –ing*); *too/enough*.

OTHER To introduce the vocabulary of job-specific clothing and equipment, and explain its precise purpose as a means of establishing basic needs and functions of different specialisms; to establish the idea of thinking in cross-sectoral terms.

Sample topic Medicine and health care; Construction and building trades

Transfer Activity can be transferred to any specialism. Clothing and equipment are important in most professions.

Materials Pictures of uniformed workers—for example, nurse, police officer, builder.

Preparation

Think about the specialism of the students you are teaching. List the clothing and equipment they need. For each item think of a similar item that is not quite right—for example, a nurse or a doctor might need surgical gloves, a similar item would be gardening gloves or washing-up gloves. If you can find realia and pictures for these items, all the better. (This preparation will help with step 6 below.)

Procedure

1 Show students three pictures of 'uniformed' workers. Ask the students to say what they are wearing, and any equipment they are carrying or might have in their pockets—for example, uniform, helmet, mask, overalls, thermometer, hammer, nails, etc.

2 Identify the purpose of each piece of clothing or equipment. Give two examples and then elicit the rest from the students.

Example *Why does he need a helmet? In order to protect his head.*
Why does she use a thermometer? It's used for taking the temperature of the patients.

3 Write example on the board and practise the vocabulary and the language of purpose.

4 Get the students to think of their own specialism. Do they wear any special clothes? Do they have any special equipment? Get students to produce a list and explain the purpose of each item. You may want to limit the list to three or four items only.

5 Show the students the two pairs of gloves. Ask them why a doctor or nurse can't use gardening or washing-up gloves, and why a gardener can't use surgical gloves. Elicit and practise appropriate language—for example, *They're too thick/thin. They can't be used for –ing.*

6 Get students to think of similar or related items for each of the items they listed for their own specialism in step 4, and discuss how they might be used differently in other specialisms.

Variation 1

For elementary students, a simpler version is a 'show and tell' activity: students bring along the most important or favourite item to 'show' the class and 'tell' why it's important.

Variation 2

For a more fun communicative activity, at the end divide the students into pairs, each taking turns to be 'shopkeeper' and 'customer'. The customer has to ask for one of the special items they need for their job and explain why he or she needs it. The shopkeeper should offer the alternative item and try to explain how it can be used instead of the requested item. Encourage the customer to accept the alternative if the shopkeeper has convincingly shown how it can fulfil the required purpose.

Follow-up

Use the language of purpose to describe and define the language needs you are planning to meet on the course.

1.5 What do you need to read?

Level Elementary to advanced

Time 30 minutes

Aims LANGUAGE Modals of obligation and necessity (*need and have to*); describing purpose.

OTHER To identify the texts used in the specialism and the particular reading skills needed, which will then help you to select appropriate texts and write appropriate tasks.

Sample topic General

Materials Realia of a variety of reading materials, for example, magazines, phone books, labels from tins, websites, forms, timetables. Include one or two that would be used in the specialism.

Preparation

1 Collect the realia described above.

2 Prepare a list of 'I need to read' statements (see step 6) on a handout or OHT, or it could simply be written on the board.

Procedure

1 Ask the students what things they read—generally rather than in their job. They may come up with conventional texts such as newspapers, books, emails.

2 Present the realia introducing other types of reading—for example, phone book, tin label, timetable, etc. Elicit other types of reading text—try to get as many as possible. Write them on the board.

3 Select two or three and ask the class *who* reads them and *why* they read them. Also ask: *How* do they read them? The class may need some help with this, so ask other questions: do they need to understand every word, or just get a general impression? Do they need to look for specific information?

4 In pairs, get the students to group the different reading texts by type. You can either get them to come up with their own categories or give them the four basic types:
   • Reading for general understanding (to get the gist)
   • Reading for detailed understanding of everything in the text
   • Reading for a specific piece of information
   • Reading for pleasure.
   Report back to the whole class.

5 Get the students to think about their own specialism and the type of reading texts they meet there, and the way they need to read them. Write the types of text and the required reading sub-skills on the board as they emerge.

Example *Reading a report to find out a specific piece of information.*

6 Hand out a list of 'I need to read' statements and get the students to decide if they are true for them. The list could be as follows, but you may want to add some of your own.

Example

> • I need to read quickly for general understanding.
> • I need to read in detail and understand the whole text.
> • I need to read to find out particular pieces of information.
> • I need to read and then write a similar text.
> • I need to read and then explain the content to a colleague or customer.
> • I need to read and then translate into my own language.
> • I need to read aloud at meetings and presentations.

Photocopiable © Oxford University Press

The answers to these statements (and the list in step 5) will provide you not only with the types of text you need to use on the course, but also—and perhaps more importantly—the types of task you need to set.

7 Finish the lesson by asking the class what they read for pleasure (in their own language). Ask them: *do these texts involve similar reading skills to the ones you identified as important for your specialism?* Are there parallel texts in English they can find for these pleasure items? For example, if they read music magazines, can they find English ones?

Variation 1

Follow the same procedure for the other language skills (listening, writing, and speaking) to identify needs, and types of text and interaction.

Variation 2

Give students a 'genre-switching' activity, where they are given two contrasting text genres, one from their specialism and one from their general life (for example, a report on a scientific experiment and an email to a friend about an exciting weekend). They write each one in the style of the other—for example, *Report on weekend activities. Equipment used: motorbike, tent, two friends etc.*

Comments

This activity leads nicely into 1.6, 'The authentic materials bank'.

1.6 The authentic materials bank

Level	All levels
Time	20–30 minutes (for the Set-up)
Aims	To establish an awareness of students' needs based on authentic materials that the students themselves bring in and contribute to on an ongoing basis; to assist the teacher with course design, and to actively involve the students in course design and materials gathering.
Sample topic	Tourism—hotel reception
Transfer	Activity can be transferred to any specialism.
Materials	Filing system for accessible storage of materials; a range of authentic materials from a variety of jobs.

Procedure

Set-up

1 Early on in the course explain to students the purpose of the 'Authentic materials bank'—namely, for students to collect and bring in examples of authentic material that they use in their specialism, so that the course can be designed to meet their needs.

2 Find out if the students have access to authentic materials—and make sure they have authorization to use them.

3 Introduce the topic of types of communication. How do people communicate in different jobs? Elicit a range of types: face-to-face, phone, email, memo, letter, report, invoices, etc. Which ones are used in their specialism? Get the students to give some actual examples.

4 Get students to complete this chart to show what you mean by 'authentic materials'. Do the example of the hotel receptionist with them in class. (This activity leads on logically from 1.5, 'What do you need to read?')

Worksheet 1.6		
Authentic material	Example: hotel receptionist	Your specialism
Reading texts	Computer reservation screens Forms in general Bills and invoices	
Spoken situations	Checking in a guest Checking out a guest Dealing with enquiries and requests Handling complaints Liaising with colleagues Speaking on the phone	
Listening needs	Understanding different accents Understanding phone messages	
Writing needs	Completing forms Sending responses to enquiries	

Photocopiable © Oxford University Press

5 Ask students to gather and bring in examples of all the authentic materials identified in their specialism. Obviously they will not be able to bring in the speaking/listening materials (although it may be possible to record things, such as phone conversations), but they can still note down the situation and the main points that were made. Set an achievable target of just one or two items for every session that you teach them.

Ongoing use of the 'Authentic materials bank'

1 When the materials start to come in, decide with the students how to organize them—for example, which categories to put them in, where to store them, etc.

2 Appoint a bank manager to be responsible for organization and maintenance of the materials. The position of bank manager should be rotated at regular intervals.

3 Use the bank yourself to prepare activities and exercises based on authentic texts and situations, and to check that the course you are delivering is meeting the real needs of the students.

4   Encourage students to borrow (or withdraw) materials from the bank to use for self-access and homework.

5   Ways of exploiting the materials will occur in the other chapters, but here are three basic exercise types that you can introduce immediately:

a   **Information gap**

Make two photocopies of the 'master' document, blank out different information on the copies (you can do this randomly, or focus on a particular information type—for example, technical vocabulary or numbers). Label one copy A and one B. You thus have two gap-fill exercises (for self-study) and one communicative information gap activity (for class use).

b   **Information transfer**

Get the students to summarize or describe the information in the authentic material in a different medium—for example, over the phone to a colleague or client, in an email, or in a report.

c   **Translation**

Get the students to translate documents in their first language into English, and documents that are in English into their first language.

Variation

Pre-work students may not have easy access to authentic materials. So set them the task of gathering material by contacting centres that provide training courses in their specialism and by visiting websites.

Comments

Apart from the initial set-up, this is not a single activity, but an ongoing source of reference during the course, to be used at regular times (depending on the course timetable). The 'bank' can be used for quick fillers, for longer class-work activities, or for self-access by the students.

1.7 The A to Z of job skills

Level Pre-intermediate to advanced

Time 50 minutes, plus 20 minutes for step 7 (this can be done as homework)

Aims LANGUAGE Talking about skills and qualifications (*have to be able to/know how to/be good at/be willing to...* etc.).

OTHER To identify specific skills and needs of different jobs and vocations; to practise the language of talking about job skills.

Sample topic Architecture and design

Transfer Activity can be transferred to any specialism.

Materials Photocopies of Worksheet 1.7—one per group.

Procedure

1 Write the letters A, B, C, D ... to Z in a column on the board. Ask students for a job beginning with A (for example, architect) and another beginning with Z (for example, zoo-keeper).

2 In groups, get students to brainstorm job names for the other letters. Aim for one for each, but it is not necessary to get one for every letter of the alphabet. Stop the brainstorming once you feel confident that there is a range of different job types—i.e. some manual, some service sector, some professional, etc. (See 'Variation' for a way of doing this activity if you want to keep it specific to your specialism.)

3 Feedback on some of the letters to check the definition of the jobs.

4 In groups, get the students to choose five of the jobs from their A to Z. The jobs should be as different from each other as possible.

5 Get the groups to complete Worksheet 1.7. Do 'architect' as an example first, in order to bring out some of the language of job skills (*You have to be able to/know how to/be willing to* ..., etc.), demonstrate what you mean by 'Language situations' and show them that they need to think about all the skills (reading, writing, listening, and speaking).

6 When the groups have completed their grid, get them to read out one of the 'Skills and qualifications' and one of the 'Language situations' at a time. See if the other groups can guess the job. If the other groups have problems guessing the job, other clues can be given, such as role-playing a dialogue with one of the language situations, miming an action, or giving the first letter.

7 To finish, get the students to complete a detailed grid entry for their own specialism or vocation. (This could then be written up as a full job description—see 2.2, 'Job descriptions and interviews'.)

Worksheet 1.7

Job	Skills and qualifications *You have to…*	Language situations
Architect	… be able to draw neatly … understand principles of engineering and science … work to deadlines … etc.	Listening to and speaking to clients (about their wishes, their proposals, etc.). Speaking to colleagues and to builders. Reading plans and instructions. Reading scientific journals. Writing plans and instructions.
1		
2		
3		
4		
5		

Photocopiable © Oxford University Press

Variation

The activity is designed to put the specialism of your students in the wider context of work and jobs in general. However, if you don't want to take this approach, you can get the students to concentrate on jobs related to their specialism (for example, in a hospital: doctor, nurse, radiographer, surgeon, porter).

Follow-up

Get students to write and design a job advertisement, listing the skills and language situations.

1.8 Identifying workplace culture

Level Intermediate to advanced

Time 40 minutes

Aims LANGUAGE generic work-based lexis, such as *colleague, line-manager, open-door, initiative*, etc., language of opinions and discussion.

OTHER To identify the internal culture of a company or workplace, so that the course can be designed to conform to this culture as much as possible.

Sample topic General—although the worksheet used here is more suited to Administration and office work, and other professional areas.

Materials Photocopies of Worksheet 1.8—one per student.

Preparation

To sensitize yourself to the activity, complete the chart for yourself, firstly for your ideal job, and secondly for the place where you actually work.

Procedure

1 Get the students to talk generally about the place where they work— *How many people share the work space? Who are they responsible to? Do they have a line manager? What's the boss like?* Use this step to pre-teach any of the vocabulary from the worksheet that you think is necessary.

Note This activity should be handled with sensitivity if you are working with people from the same company or department, where there may be internal politics and even some discontent. If you feel you are getting into dangerous and sensitive areas, get the students to complete Worksheet 1.8 on their own as a homework exercise, with a guarantee that their answers will be confidential and will simply be used by you to help plan the course. If not, continue as follows.

2 Give out Worksheet 1.8 and ask the students to complete it on their own for their ideal job (i.e. not necessarily the job they are doing now). They should put a mark on the line between each pair of statements, depending on how close they feel to them. At the end they should draw a line connecting the different points.

3 Now get the students to complete the worksheet for the job they are actually doing. Again, they should draw a connecting line (in a different colour) at the end.

4 In pairs, get the students to show their completed sheets to each other. Are the two lines close to each other or far apart? Do they have similar results to their partner?

5 Group feedback. Find out who has lines that are very close to each other, and who has lines that are far apart. *What does this mean?* (Obviously, if the lines are close together, then the student should be happy in their job as their ideal job conforms to the culture of their actual job.)

6 Further discussion. You can take this discussion as far as you want. For example, you might want to discuss whether the existing workplace culture could or should be changed, whether different cultures are suitable for different jobs, and so on.

Worksheet 1.8
Your ideal job and your actual job

I meet with my line manager by appointment only	My line manager has an 'open-door' policy
I am not encouraged to take initiative	I am encouraged to take initiative
Everyone has their own separate work space	The work environment is communal
The boss makes all the decisions	Decisions are made collectively through consultation
I am told what to do	I am involved in project-planning
My colleagues don't socialize much after work	My colleagues regularly meet for social events
There is not much variety in my daily/ weekly routine	I do different things every day/week
I work on one task at a time	I have to 'multi-task' —do more than one thing at the same time.
There aren't many opportunities for promotion	There is a good career structure with promotion opportunities
I can work flexible hours and take time off when I want	My hours and holiday dates are fixed

Photocopiable © Oxford University Press

Needs analysis and course design | **33**

Variation

For lower levels, you can keep to simpler concepts (for example, likes and dislikes: *I like/don't like to start work early. I like/don't like to have a long lunch break,* etc.).

Follow-up

Get students to write a proposal about how their working environment could be changed to make it more suited to their own desires and working style.

1.9 The classroom as workplace

Level Elementary to advanced

Time 30 minutes

Aims LANGUAGE Question forms; comparing and contrasting.

OTHER To relate the language learning experience to the working experience, and think of ways in which the classroom can replicate the culture of the specialism.

Sample topic General

Preparation

None, unless you want to put the topics listed in step 2 on a worksheet with two columns next to them, one headed 'Classroom' and one headed 'Workplace'.

Procedure

1 Ask the students generally how the classroom where they are studying is different from the place where they work.

2 Get the students, either in pairs, groups, or whole class (or a mixture), to think about each of the following aspects of their learning/working environment. For each question, get them to think about the classroom first and then the workplace. After each one, write the main points on the board.

Example
- What is the size, shape, atmosphere, and lighting like in the room?
- What's on the walls?
- What are the work-stations like (for example, desks, labs, etc.)?
- What equipment and machinery is there in the room?
- What materials are used and how do you work with them?
- Who is in the room? What are their roles?
- What interactions take place? Who talks to whom, and how do they talk?
- What language is used?
- How much time is spent in the room? Are there any breaks?

3 Input some language of comparatives, using the first question as an example. Remember to include comparative 'linkers' such as *whereas* or *on the one hand … on the other hand,* not just adjectives.

4   Get students to compare the differences for all the other questions. How different are the two settings? What similarities are there?

5   Feedback on the differences and similarities. In course planning and in future lessons, bear in mind these differences. For example, if the workplace interaction is mainly in teams or pairs, then use group work or pair work more in classroom activities.

6   Discuss with the group if anything in the classroom could be adjusted to make it more like the workplace—for example, re-arranging the furniture, putting something else on the wall. Ask students if they would like to do this—they may not want to, as they may prefer their classroom to 'look like a classroom' (but even so, it will be useful when practising language in situations to be able to simulate certain features of the workplace).

Variation

If the students come from different companies (or even different specialisms), get them to compare their different working environments first.

1.10   Identifying target events

Level   All levels

Time   45–50 minutes

Aims   To design a detailed framework for the whole ESP course, incorporating target events, skills areas, language work, materials, and classroom activities; to involve students in the ordering and organization of the course.

Sample topic   Tourism—travel agents

Transfer   Activity can be transferred to any specialism.

Materials   A large-scale presentation chart (or interactive whiteboard if available).

Preparation

1   Carry out a needs analysis with the students (for example, 1.2, 'What do you need?' combined with any of the other activities in this chapter), in order to produce a comprehensive list of target events.

Example   *For travel agents this would include:*
- welcoming clients and making them feel relaxed
- writing emails to confirm booking arrangements
- booking airline tickets through a CRS (Computerized Reservations System).

Try to keep the list to a maximum of 20 key target events (with less important events kept in reserve). At this stage do not worry about the order of the target events.

2 Produce a large grid or chart—either on paper or, if you will have access to an interactive whiteboard in the classroom, on computer. The chart should have nine rows, as in the example below (using the three target events for the travel agents).

The last two rows ('Importance' and 'Order') should be left empty. There may be other spaces where there is nothing relevant to put.

You should make use of any in-house or external syllabuses that you have to work to, as well as the information arising from the 'Needs analysis' activities. This document will require a lot of time to produce, so you may want to work on it over a period of time before and during the early stages of the course. It will however be an extremely valuable document throughout the course, so it is worth doing it thoroughly.

3 Think about the order in which you might present the items during the course, but do not make any definitive conclusions. You will need to order the target events according to three main criteria:
   • when they are needed in the specialism
   • the complexity of language required
   • external and institutional constraints (such as examinations).

Procedure

1 Establish with the students what are the important criteria for a successful course. The following points could be put on to a worksheet or simply elicited and boarded for discussion and ranking:

Example   A successful course …
   • is comprehensive (it covers all the areas)
   • develops logically (for example, in terms of language complexity)
   • has variety (for example, it doesn't have six lessons in a row on writing).
   • is interesting and relevant to our specialism
   • leads to competence and qualifications
   • can be adapted as we go along.

2 Present the chart of target events with the nine columns. Ask the students if any target events are missing, and add them if necessary. (It may be a good idea to deliberately miss out one key target event so that students can identify it and build the other column entries in order to understand the thinking behind the columns.)

3 In groups, get students to decide on the 'Importance' column, by evaluating how important the target event is for their needs and giving it a score from 1–5 (1 = not very important; 5 = very important).

4 Feedback to the whole group and try to reach a consensus on levels of importance.

Target events/Course design (with example of travel agents)			
	Target event		
	Welcoming clients and making them feel relaxed	Writing emails to confirm booking arrangements	Booking airline tickets through a CRS (Computerized Reservations System)
Skills	Speaking	Writing	Using computers (reading and interacting with computer screens)
Function	Welcoming; Being polite; Offers	Giving information	Inputting and processing information
Language area	Indirect question forms; Would you like?	Vocabulary of tickets, booking, confirmation. Email conventions	Dates, numbers, details
Materials	N/A	Tickets Booking forms Computer	Computer CRS software
Interaction	Teacher presentation Dialogue Role-play	Text analysis Pair work Text production	Teacher presentation Simulation
Related areas	Identifying client needs; Customer service	Other emails to clients; Internal emails; Telephoning to confirm	Confirming reservations; Completing forms (paper and electronic)
Importance			
Order			

Photocopiable © Oxford University Press

5 Divide the class in half.
   - Group A should order the target events according to when they need to cover them in terms of the logic of their specialism (i.e. regardless of language complexity or interconnection). They can refer to a subject (i.e. non-language) coursebook or training manual. You may need to help pre-work students with this.
   - Group B should order the target events according to the language level and complexity. They can compare with the contents page of a General English coursebook.

   The main idea is to get the students thinking generally about the criteria of 'order' in an ESP course.

6 Regroup with two As and two Bs. Try to agree on an order.

7 Get the groups to report back to the whole class. Introduce into the whole-class discussion elements such as review, progress testing, homework, project assignments, and coursework, and consider how all of them will fit into the course design. You will also need to relate the course design to the course timetable—the length of course, how often you meet, how many lessons you have, etc.

8 At this stage the classroom work is complete. Tell the class that you will now use their thoughts and discussion points to produce a definitive version, which you will print out and give to them. When producing the definitive version make sure you include space and flexibility and the opportunity for adjustment.

9 Revisit the course design on a regular basis (both with the class and on your own) to ensure it is meeting everyone's needs. It can also be used as a basis for testing and evaluation activities (see Chapter 8).

Comments

1 As it stands, this activity is very lengthy, time-consuming, and ongoing. This is because we have assumed that the teacher is starting from scratch. In many situations this will not be the case as there may be a pre-existing course plan and an externally imposed syllabus. Nevertheless, the basic activities described here can be used to test any such plans and syllabuses and make sure they are meeting the true needs of the specialism.

2 For elementary students the course plan will need to be less grandiose, but it can nevertheless focus on immediate needs and a limited range of specific target events.

2

Organizational structures

Organizations can have very different internal structures, depending on factors such as the nature of the specialism, the size of the operation, and the location. The main purpose of the activities in this chapter is to examine this internal structure, the way the organization knits together, and the lines of communication and interaction. In so doing we are exploring the internal culture of the specialism, identified in Chapter 1, in a more detailed and analytical way.

Organograms (see 2.1, 'Organograms')—diagrams and models of the internal structure of an organization—are often used to represent how an organization works. Looking at different organograms and producing one for the students' own specialism and their own company or workplace is a useful starting point, although obviously there is no standard organogram for each specialism and they will differ from workplace to workplace. As in Chapter 1, the idea is to get students to think across sectors, and to see their own specialism in the context of, and in contrast to, other forms of workplace organization. It is often easier to understand how one's own organization operates and is structured when you step outside of it.

In order to understand the organizational structure of a specialism or a workplace it is useful to focus on particular micro elements:

- the role of an individual, for example through a job description (2.2, 'Job descriptions and interviews')
- the way a vital piece of equipment is used within the organization (2.3, 'The photocopier')
- the way in which instructions are given and day-to-day duties are tackled (2.4, 'Instruction dictation' and 2.5, '"To do" lists').

This linking of the detail of internal organization with the bigger picture of organizational structure is a theme throughout the chapter, and culminates with the two final larger-scale activities (2.6, 'Organizing a trade fair and conference' and 2.7, 'Job swap').

2.1 Organograms

Level Elementary to advanced

Time 30–40 minutes

Aims LANGUAGE Vocabulary of jobs and workplace relationships—verbs and nouns.

OTHER To look at organization charts (organograms) in different specialisms and compare with students' own specialism and place of work.

Sample topic Construction and building trades—hotels and hospitals are used as contrast.

Transfer Activity can be transferred to any specialism. It doesn't matter if students don't know the right answer—the main point is to discuss working organizations before relating them to their own specialism in steps 6 and 7.

Materials Photocopies of an organogram and organizational model (for step 5)—one per student; some pictures of jobs in the trades you have chosen.

Preparation

1 Photocopy the example organogram (and the diagram of organizational models, if you are including step 5).

2 Research an organogram for a company involved in the specialism you are teaching.

Procedure

1 Set the scene by asking: *who works in a hotel, in a hospital, or on a construction site?* Although these may not be the students' own specialisms, they should be able to identify with them and have some experience of them as organizations. Use pictures if necessary.

2 Ask students to organize the different jobs for each of the three areas in any way they feel appropriate. This will be easier if you have used pictures (with or without the names of the jobs) on small pieces of paper or card.

3 Focus on the construction trade. Give out the organogram. Get the students to look at the key features:
  • Who's in charge?
  • Are there different departments?
  • Who supervises who?
  • Is everyone directly employed (as opposed to sub-contracted)?

4 Get the students to attempt to produce similar organograms for the hotel and the hospital.

5 (Optional) Introduce the diagram of organizational models and ask which of the models is most similar to the ones they produced in step 4.

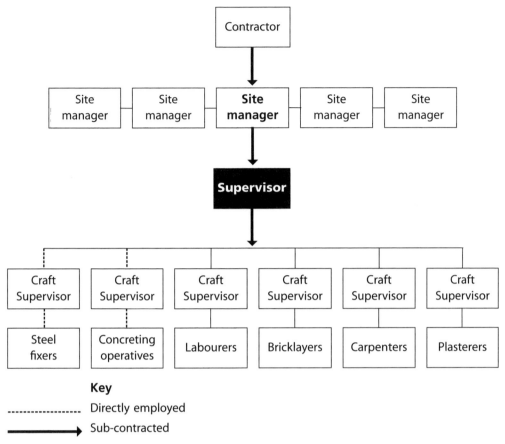

ABC Construction Ltd

Key

- - - - - - - - - - Directly employed

→ Sub-contracted

Photocopiable © Oxford University Press

6 Relate the three organograms (and the organizational models in step 5, if included) to the students' own organization, by asking:
- Which organogram is closest to your own organization or company?
- What is the position closest to yours in each of the organograms?

7 Get the students in pairs or groups to produce their own organogram for their organization or company. Compare with other groups.

Variation 1

For elementary students, substitute pictures for names (or use labelled pictures)—for example: *bricklayer, carpenter, site supervisor, site manager* in the construction organogram. Such pictures are usually easily downloaded from an image search engine like Google.

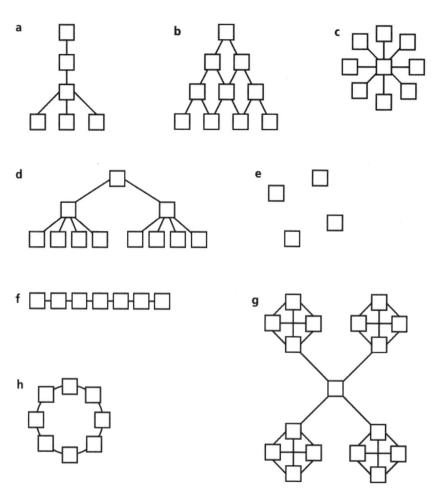

Photocopiable © Oxford University Press

Variation 2

Use children's building blocks as an alternative way of constructing models to represent students' organizations. Students do this freely and then explain the thinking behind their models to other students. Alternatively, use a pack of cards plus adhesive putty.

Follow-up

The activity leads into the next activity—2.2, 'Job descriptions and interviews'.

2.2 Job descriptions and interviews

Level	Pre-intermediate to advanced	
Time	50–60 minutes	
Aims	LANGUAGE	Modals (*must, should, can*); phrases describing job skills/requirements (*good with/at, ability to, willing to,* etc.).
	OTHER	To look at the language of job descriptions.
Sample topic	General	
Transfer	Activity can be transferred to any specialism, but there may be a different style and content in different specialisms—for example, more emphasis may be put on actual qualifications in professional specialisms; customer-based specialisms may stress interpersonal qualities, etc.	
Materials	Photocopies of a job description from the specialism—one per student.	

Procedure

1 In pairs, get students to think about the job of teacher (or some other universally recognized job, President of the USA often works quite well!).

Ask them to think about:
- duties and responsibilities
- skills and qualities needed (essential or desirable?)
- qualifications (essential or desirable?)
- the terms and conditions (hours, salary, benefits).

2 Feedback on the ideas and board them in four columns, one for each of the areas identified above.

3 Teach the language of job descriptions:

Example You must/should be good with/good at …
You must be able to/willing to …
You must/should have the ability to/a willingness to …
The job involves …
The following minimum qualifications are required …
There are 24 days' paid holiday.
The salary is …

4 Get students to write a job description either for their own job, or, if they are pre-work, for their ideal job. They should use the four headings from step 1.

5 Give out the authentic example from the specialism and ask students to compare. They can make any changes to the description they wrote.

6 Get the students to swap their job descriptions with a partner, and then take turns to interview each other—in effect, for their own jobs. Encourage interviewees to ask questions as well (they will actually know more about the job description, as they wrote it). Allow a little preparation time before the interview.

Variation

Convert the example job description into an information gap activity, by copying it twice and deleting different information from the two copies. Students have to ask their partner for the missing information.

Follow-up

Write an advertisement for the job. (Bring in some examples of job advertisements as a guide.)

2.3 The photocopier

Level	Pre-intermediate to advanced
Time	30–40 minutes
Aims LANGUAGE	Instructions: imperatives, can; passive; second conditional (for stage 4)
OTHER	To examine organizational structures and instructions by focusing on a key piece of equipment and how it is used in the organization.
Sample topic	Administration and office work
Transfer	Activity can be transferred to any specialism. Try to select a piece of equipment that is not only important to the job, but is as technically-sophisticated as possible.
Materials	Photocopies of Worksheet 2.3, 'The company photocopier—important information'.

Preparation

1 Think about a key piece of equipment that is used in the specialism you are teaching—this is in addition to the photocopier example used at the start of the activity.

2 Adapt Worksheet 2.3 to conform to actual practice in your organization, as far as possible. If you feel a photocopier is totally out of your students' sphere of understanding, then use another piece of generic equipment, such as a coffee machine.

3 Copy the worksheet, either in its correct final version or with the various bullet points jumbled up.

Procedure

1 Introduce the photocopier (either by a picture, the word on the board, or the item itself if it is near), and write four headings on the board:

- Who uses it?
- How do you use it?
- How do you look after it?
- Who's responsible for it?

2 Elicit the various instructions and conditions of use as below. Alternatively, give out the worksheet with the bullet points all jumbled up and get students to match them to the correct heading.

Worksheet 2.3

The company photocopier

Important information

Who uses it?
- The copier can be used by all members of staff.
- Staff can only use it for work-related business.
- It cannot be used by non-employees without the special permission of a manager.

How do you use it?
- Enter your PIN number.
- Place your original on the glass.
- Select the size and quantity you require, and press start.
- Do not waste paper by making unnecessary copies.
- Use the double-sided and leaflet options when appropriate.
- Use the recycling bin for waste paper.

How do you look after it?
- Keep the area of the photocopier clean and tidy.
- Do not force or pull paper through the machine if there is a paper jam.
- Report any malfunction to the person responsible (see below).

Who's responsible for it?
- The photocopier is leased from and serviced by AMS Ltd.
- If there are any problems with the machine please inform the Maintenance Dept or your line manager as soon as possible.

Photocopiable © Oxford University Press

3 Get students to think of a key piece of equipment needed in their specialism and organization (for example, computer, lathe, etc.). Get them to produce a similar set of instructions and conditions of use, using the four headings (or adapting if applicable).

4 Discuss how the organization would manage if the piece of key equipment didn't exist, or had broken down, or been stolen. What internal changes would be needed to deal with the work? Get the students to devise a contingency plan for this eventuality. (This idea is expanded in 4.6, 'Living without it'.)

Variation 1

If you want to focus explicitly on instruction giving and receiving, then concentrate on the 'How do you use it?' part of the activity, and get students giving each other instructions on a piece of equipment, either face-to-face or over the phone (i.e. with or without the actual piece of equipment before them).

Variation 2

If you want to focus more on the structure of the organization, then concentrate on exactly who uses the equipment and for which specific tasks. This will inform the final stage more directly.

Follow-up

Role-play the induction of a new employee in how to use the photocopier (or other piece of equipment).

2.4 Instruction dictation

Level	Elementary to advanced	
Time	30–40 minutes	
Aims	LANGUAGE	Modals (*should, ought to, must, have to*); sequencers (*first, then, next, finally*, etc.).
	OTHER	To develop fluency, note-taking, and peer-listening skills when briefing a colleague.
Sample topic	General	
Transfer	Activity can be used with any specialism. You can adapt the text format so that it is in the same genre as texts used in the specialism—for example, a memo or an email.	
Materials	Texts on paper and a means of sticking them on the wall.	

Preparation

Write a text giving briefing notes for a new colleague on the procedures to follow at the start of the day. Use the specialism if you know enough about it. If you don't, you can make the text about a teacher:

Example *First you have to check in with the Director of Studies to find out if there are any class changes or other important information. Check the noticeboard as well. Then you should …*, etc.

Depending on the size of your class, you may need more than one copy of the text.

Procedure

1 Divide the class into pairs. One student in each pair is the 'runner' and the other student is the 'writer'.

2 Pin up the text on a wall.

3 Tell the runners to go and read the text and report back one line at a time to the writer. The runners are not allowed to write anything down, but must remember and relate the lines as accurately as possible (including punctuation).

4 The winning team is the first team to get a complete text, with time penalties added for inaccuracies.

5 At the end, check that students have fully understood the text.

6 Get the students to write a parallel text, either for their own specialism if you used the teacher example, or for briefing on 'end of day' procedures if you used their specialism. Check that the texts are accurate.

7 Redistribute the texts and repeat the running dictation activity, reversing the role of the runners and writers.

Variation 1

For pre-work students the text can be about their start of day procedures at school or college, or it could be about the stages they will go through to begin work or training in the specialism (for example, *First I have to prepare a good CV ...*).

Variation 2

For advanced level students you can increase the length and complexity of the text at the same time as reducing the time allowed. Also be rigorous about correct punctuation and accuracy in general.

Follow-up

1 Compare and discuss the start of day (and end of day) procedures at the students' workplace, and whether any improvements or efficiencies can be made.

2 Write briefing notes for other parts of the job.

3 Discuss how new colleagues are briefed and trained in their specialism.

2.5 'To do' lists

Level Elementary to advanced

Time 30 minutes (longer if step 6—inputting language—is required)

Aims LANGUAGE Lexis of job tasks relevant to your students' specialism; language of making requests and asking for a favour; telephone language.

OTHER To practise making and prioritizing lists of tasks.

Sample topic General

Transfer Activity can be used with any specialism. It will have relevance wherever there are co-workers.

Preparation

Prepare examples of your own 'To do' lists—for today, next week, next month. Try to make the tasks mainly, but not exclusively, professional—for example, *mark homework, prepare end of course test, take cat to the vet.*

Procedure

1 Write your 'To do' lists on the board or OHP. Ask students how they remember what they have to do (for example, on post-its, on computer, etc.).

2 Involve students in deciding what your priorities are. Number them according to class consensus.

3 Get students to write their own 'To do' lists—for today, next week, and next month. On the whole they should be work-related, but they can include one or two that are personal.

4 Get the students to decide the priority for their tasks.

5 Refer students back to your lists. Say that there's been an emergency and you've got to go away immediately. Who can you ask to do your tasks? Again, involve the class in the decisions.

6 Get students to do the same with their own lists. If necessary, teach/revise the language of making requests and asking a favour (and the responses), and telephoning language.

7 In pairs, the students to role-play the requests.

8 Pairs feedback to class. How successful were they in delegating their tasks? Did the other student understand exactly what they had to do?

Variation 1

For pre-work students the focus can be on how they organize their study/coursework tasks (or their domestic tasks).

Variation 2

Instead of making the requests and giving the instructions over the phone, get the students to write emails or notes to their colleagues. You can then focus on the contrasting style of different communication media.

Variation 3

Instead of asking colleagues and peers, get the students to ask superiors and subordinates. Again, this will give you the opportunity to look at contrasting registers.

Follow-up

1 Encourage students to maintain ongoing 'To do' lists in English, for their job and for their English studies.

2 Get students to write up the requests and instructions as formal briefing notes to a colleague (in a format appropriate to their specialism).

2.6 Organizing a trade fair and conference

Level Intermediate to advanced

Time 60 minutes for basic activity. But could be longer and can be developed over several sessions (see ideas in Variations and Follow-up).

Aims LANGUAGE Making suggestions; agreeing and disagreeing.

OTHER To carry out a simulation to organize a trade fair and conference; to encourage students to think about the organization, structure, and lines of responsibility and communication of their specialism.

Sample topic Tourism and travel

Transfer Activity can be transferred to any specialism by stressing different aspects of the organization in step 3, for example, budgets or customer care.

Materials Authentic examples of trade fairs and conferences for the specialism (if available).

Preparation

Try to find actual examples of trade fairs and conferences for the specialism you are teaching to serve as a model and a check on the authenticity of what the students produce. This will be especially important for pre-work students.

Procedure

1 Set the scene. Tell the students they are going to be planning and hosting a trade fair or a conference for their specialism in the town or city where they are studying. The main focus of the event should be related to the internal organization and structure of their specialism—something like: 'How can we work together as an industry?' In Tourism, for example, this would mean looking at strategies to integrate and cooperate with the different sectors (tour operation, travel agencies and retail, transport, accommodation, tourist information, and government tourist boards). For pre-work students it might be best to focus on one aspect of the specialism—for example, finding work in a hotel.

2　Get the class to agree on 'global' issues:
- the size of the event
- what to include
- who to invite
- the venue
- how many days.

3　Divide the class into groups to work on practical arrangements. How you do this will depend on the size of the class you are teaching. Ideally you should have six groups to work on each of the suggested areas, but you can combine if necessary, or focus only on one or two of the suggested areas.

Suggested areas:
- organizing the venue
- agenda and schedule (for both the conference and the fair)
- invitations (including VIPs, guest speakers)
- staffing, security, and catering
- entertainment and hospitality
- budget.

4　In groups, students plan for the event and decide what needs to be done. They then draw up an action plan and allocate roles to *all* the class members (not just the members of their group), depending on their perceived abilities, skills, and knowledge.

5　Once the action plan and role allocation is complete, get the students to go round and ask the class members if they can do the task that's been allocated. This stage will be somewhat chaotic and should resemble a rather frantic recruitment 'market place', so help to manage this by moving furniture, asking students to speak quietly, and so on.

6　Students return to their groups and revise their plans and role allocation in the light of the reactions they got in step 5.

7　With the class as a whole, finalize planning arrangements on the board. In particular come up with:
- structure and personnel for the main organizing committee
- outline of the agenda and schedule
- action plan and budget
- briefs and instructions for all class members.

Variation

Spread the different steps over a series of sessions, one step at a time. This will have the advantage of not only breaking up the activity into more manageable chunks, but also allowing time to research and develop each step. In this way it could be an ongoing coursework project.

Follow-up

1　Students write a schedule and agenda, produce a business plan, and design some promotional information for the event.

2   The ultimate 'Follow-up' activity would be to actually hold the event, if not in its entirety then perhaps for the other students in the institution.

2.7 Job swap

Level   Intermediate to advanced

Time   50 minutes

Aims   LANGUAGE   Daily routines (present simple); giving instructions.

OTHER   To practise language of instruction in relation to routines and tasks (at work and at home) and to encourage active listening skills and note-taking.

Sample topic   General

Transfer   Activity can be used with any specialism. Build in functions that are needed in the specialism you are teaching, for example, requests, recommendations, or directions.

Preparation

Be sure you know about the work situation of the students.

Procedure

1   Set the scene. Each student is taking part in a 'job exchange' with a student who has a different job. He or she will work in the office, workshop, or other type of workplace of their partner. They will sit at their desk or work-station, and carry out their tasks and duties.

2   In whole class discuss generally what things are important in a job exchange like this, and what you would worry about and want to know.

3   Instruct the students, on their own, to write down the information they need to give to their exchange partner. Put prompts on board:

Example   • work
   • daily routine, with times (and breaks)
   • start of day and end of day tasks
   • other important tasks
   • important information about colleagues
   • where things are (for example, in desk, office, workshop, etc.).

Students should include advice and warnings as well as instructions.

4   Pair up the students and get them to exchange information. The 'instructors' should not show the information they wrote down in step 3 above. Make sure that the 'listeners' make notes and ask for clarification. At the end the 'instructor' should check the notes that the 'listener' has made to make sure nothing has been missed.

5   Swap the roles of 'instructor' and 'listener'.

6 Whole class feedback. Ask some general questions:
  • Do you feel confident that your exchange partner will do a good job?
  • Is there anything you are worried about?
  • Do you think your job is easier than your partner's?
  • Has the experience made you see your job differently?

Variation 1

For elementary students, you can keep to just one aspect of the exchange—for example, just a 'desk-swap'.

Variation 2

To add an extra dimension to the activity you could include a 'home exchange', whereby partners will live in each other's homes as well.

Example
  • where things are
  • how the electricity, heating, etc. works
  • what to do about security
  • the neighbours
  • local facilities.

This could be the main focus for pre-work students.

Variation 3

The activity works best if all the students work for different companies, or different branches of the same company, or if they have completely different jobs. If they all work at the same place, the activity will still work, but you may want to get them to use previous jobs (or the job of a close friend or family member) in order to maximise interest and the sense of 'information gap'.

Follow-up

It may be possible, through international connections of professional associations or through multinational companies themselves, to get in touch with people who do similar jobs to your students in English speaking countries. If it is, then you could get your students to write to them and do a 'virtual exchange'—in other words find out about daily routines, tasks, and what their job (and lifestyle) is like. It could even lead to *actual* exchanges.

3

Vocabulary

Vocabulary is an important part of the ESP course. Partly this is because specific technical words are used to describe particular features of the specialism—for example, the components of a car engine for motor mechanics—and these have to be known in order to function in the specialism. But sometimes semi-technical vocabulary can be just as problematic. In Academic English and in Business, Management and IT these are words such as: *factor, method, function, occur, cycle, relevant, significant,* etc. Semi-technical vocabulary can include enabling and linking lexis, often occurring as groups of words—*as a result of, the report clearly shows, once the needle has been inserted, no visit to (London) is complete without, I'd like to hand over to (Liz) now,* to take some examples from random specialisms.

As well as building and practising technical and semi-technical lexis, vocabulary teaching in ESP will involve a number of sub-skills: deducing meaning from context, word-building, understanding appropriate register and genre (including formal vs informal, receptive vs productive use). Successful vocabulary learning will also involve using strategies for storing and retrieving lexical items, and research and referencing skills. These principles underlie the activities in this chapter.

Teaching and learning vocabulary is an ongoing process, and will occur in most lessons. Some of the suggested activities in this chapter are also meant to be ongoing (for example, 3.1, 'Personal learning dictionaries' and 3.2, 'Word stew'). 3.3, 'Abbreviation and acronym Scrabble', to 3.7, 'Genre switch' provide a variety of ways of building technical specialist vocabulary and will also involve semi-technical vocabulary.

The increasing use of computer-based corpora and concordances in English Language Teaching clearly has a special relevance to ESP, allowing for accurate awareness and analysis of lexical usage in particular specialist contexts. 3.8, 'Corpora' suggests a number of ways of exploiting corpora (for example, looking at collocation and ways of deducing meaning from context), and also places them in the context of other research and reference sources.

Perhaps it is an obvious final point, but as with all aspects of ESP teaching, the needs of the students and the way the language is applied in their specialism is crucial. It is important to ensure that the students are learning and using words that they will actually need in their specialism.

3.1 Personal learning dictionaries

Level All levels

Time 40–50 minutes

Aims LANGUAGE General lexical work—for example, morphology, meaning, context, phonology.

OTHER To establish a learning strategy for storing and retrieving specialist vocabulary, which students can adapt to their personal style and needs.

Sample topic Law; Construction and building trades

Transfer Activity can be transferred to any specialism.

Materials File cards—3 or 4 per student to get them started. (If students have access to computers, set this up as a Word template.)

Preparation

Prepare a 'Personal learning dictionary' template, as described in step 4, with three or four key words from the specialism to use as a model.

Procedure

1 Present the entry from an English-English dictionary for a keyword in the specialism either on the board or copied onto a piece of paper (or computer screen). For example, 'legal' if you are teaching English for Law, 'construct' if you are teaching English for the Construction and building trades.

2 Ask the students to identify how many different pieces of information are given. For 'legal' in the Oxford Wordpower dictionary, for example, the answer is six: spelling, pronunciation, part of speech, definition, example sentence, opposite.

3 Ask students if there is any other information that would be useful to have. Elicit: translation, related words from same root ('legalize', 'legal action'), topically or situationally related words ('lawyer', 'criminal')—and anything else they come up with.

4 Get students to produce a template for their 'Personal learning dictionary' (PLD), which should include the following:
   - spelling
   - pronunciation (phonetic transcript and stress)
   - part of speech
   - grammar information (for example, countable or uncountable)
   - definition in english
   - use in an example sentence (which will be memorable for them)
   - translation into first language
   - related words from same root (include prefixes and suffixes)
   - related words from same topic/lexical area (and collocations)
   - any other information they feel is important (for example, a grade for how important they think the word is, a picture of it, whether it's more useful for comprehension or production, etc.)

The important thing is that the students should personalize their templates and add anything that will (a) be relevant to the way they will need the word, and (b) help them to retain the word.

5 Get the students to think of three other words they have learnt recently that are related to their specialism.

6 Get them to use the template to make separate file cards (either on paper/card or on computer) for each word. They can compare their cards with other students.

7 Close this part of the activity by telling students to keep adding to the PLD as an ongoing process, which will in effect lead to the production of a full technical glossary.

8 As a final step, or in a separate activity, show the students how they can use the cards as a tool for learning and revision. Here are some suggestions:

Examples a *Order the cards in different ways*
- Situationally—for example, hand-held building site equipment (trowel, wheelbarrow, hammer) vs construction equipment (scaffold, ladder, safety guard).
- Semantically—for example, cause and effect (lead to, result in, produce) vs sequencing (first of all, followed by, subsequently).
- Alphabetically (this form of ordering should perhaps not be over-emphasized).

b *Self-test and peer-test activities*
- Shuffle the cards and randomly check meaning
- Take a few cards to look at on a bus ride
- Leave cards lying around your house, to be discovered accidentally
- Test another student about what's on their cards

c *Production tasks*
- Choose eight of the cards at random and try to write a sentence (or a very short memo) containing them all.
- Have a general conversation with a friend and try to use one word from your PLD in every exchange (B can't speak until he/she recognizes a PLD word in A's utterance, and vice versa).

Variation 1

Use different coloured cards or print to help store the PLD entries. As a group work activity they can discuss the best system to use—or explain the personal system they have adopted.

Variation 2

The PLD could be made into a class dictionary (or corpus), either kept on computer files or in an index card box.

Follow-up

Continue to remind students to maintain their PLDs for new words they encounter. Have the occasional focus slot in a lesson where you look at their PLDs and compare with each other.

3.2 Word stew

Level All levels

Time 5–30 minutes

Aims To provide an ongoing resource for vocabulary revision and practice.

Sample topic General

Materials A cooking pot (to maintain the 'stew' metaphor)—or a container relevant to the specialism—for example, a tool box for manual trades, a first aid box for nursing, a briefcase for business people, and so on; cards to write words on (blank cards or pieces of paper).

Preparation

Have the box (or cooking pot) and blank cards available in every lesson.

Procedure

Ongoing procedure

1 Whenever new items of vocabulary are encountered write them on a card and add them to the pot. Remember to include phrases as well as single words.

2 You may want to start the pot off with around 100 words and phrases.

3 Encourage students to contribute to the pot.

4 It doesn't matter if there are duplicates. Indeed this may well reflect the level of importance of different words—and act as a very rough vocabulary 'corpus'.

Suggested activities

From time to time dip into the pot and pull out a dozen or so of the cards for groups of students to work with. There are two basic activity types, but you may be able to invent your own:

1 Assemble the cards randomly and have students produce a text (written or spoken) relevant to their specialism. The students can add any extra words or phrases they need, which can of course be returned to the pot at the end of the activity.

2 Whenever you are working on a particular text type or encounter (for example, a report, a dialogue, an email) use the selected words to provide material for practising production of the text or encounter. Again, words and phrases can be added if necessary.

Note In both of these suggestions, students should be allowed to reject words that they feel do not fit the text. This is an important part of relating words to the appropriate genre and register of a text or exchange.

The pot can also be used as a warmer or filler.

Example
- Pull out cards and, without showing them, elicit them from the class.
- Pull out cards and get students to use them in a complete sentence.
- Pull out cards and get students to elicit them from each other, or as part of a 'Pictionary'-style game, or 'Hangman'.
- Use the cards for random pronunciation work.

Variation

Stick the words on small magnets (for example, use a set of magnetic fridge poetry). Although time-consuming to prepare, it makes for a more fun way of using the lexical items in the class (provided you have a metal surface somewhere) or even for the students to use in their own homes (on their own fridges).

Follow-up

'Clean the pot'. As a whole class activity, pour out the contents of the pot periodically (for example, at the end of a term, or before an exam), and get them to organize and categorize the contents. This can serve as a team-building or group-bonding activity. You can also take this opportunity to throw out items that you feel are unnecessary.

3.3 Abbreviation and acronym Scrabble ®

Level	All levels
Time	20–30 minutes
Aims	LANGUAGE Pronunciation of alphabet.
	OTHER To practise typical abbreviations and acronyms of the specialism.
Sample topic	Administration and office work; Business and commerce
Transfer	Activity can be transferred to any specialism which generates sector-specific abbreviations and acronyms.
Materials	Scrabble tiles—the board is not needed. (If you don't have Scrabble tiles, you can just write out a range of letters on pieces of card—skewed to the abbreviations and acronyms that you think will occur in your specialism.)

Preparation

1 Have a technical dictionary to hand (or a general dictionary with a good abbreviations section).
2 Prepare a bag full of Scrabble tiles.

Procedure

1 Get students to brainstorm two or three abbreviations or acronyms that are used in their specialism. For example, plc, CEO, asap, PA, Co.

2 Divide into groups of 5–6, and give each group a bag of tiles/letters. Students can work as individuals or in pairs within the group to maximise communication.

3 Each student takes seven tiles. In turn they try to make an abbreviation or acronym and place it in front of them. It only counts if they can say what it stands for and how it is related to the specialism. They take replacement letters from the bag. If they can't go, they can swap some of their letters for letters in the bag.

4 The play continues either until all the letters have gone or until a pre-arranged time has been reached. The winner is the player who has made the most abbreviations and acronyms. If you want, you can use the individual letter scores that occur on the scrabble tiles.

Variation 1

Allow the students to 'make and take'—in other words they can take letters from some of their opponent's abbreviations that have already been declared.

Variation 2

If students can't go, they can use their letters to invent an acronym related to their specialism—for example, ASFM (Automatic Spam Filtering Mechanism), CM (Coffee Machine). This will have the incidental effect of practising related lexis.

Follow-up

Get the students to build up a list or glossary of technical abbreviations and acronyms.

3.4 Word steps

Level	Intermediate to advanced
Time	30 minutes
Aims	LANGUAGE Morphology, prefixes and suffixes.
	OTHER To practise word-building, in particular prefixes and suffixes.
Sample topic	Marketing and advertising
Transfer	Activity can be transferred to any specialism.
Materials	Cards with prefixes, suffixes, and root words, plus some blanks—about 20 cards per person (duplicates are allowed).

Preparation

Write a variety of affixes on separate cards—for example, *in-, un-, re-, dis-, ab-, im-, in-, under-, over-, -ly, -tion, -ment, -less, -ness, -able, -tory*, etc. Also write some root words related to the specialism. For Marketing and advertising these might be: *satisfaction, enjoy, happy, comfortable, pleased, disappointed, delight, suitable, content, agree, help, sufficient*. It doesn't matter if some of these words already have affixes.

Procedure

1   Write a root word on the board which is important in the specialism, and which can be changed by adding prefixes, suffixes, etc.

Example   In *Marketing and advertising* the word might be 'satisfaction'.

2   Get the students to give you as many words as possible from the root word: *satisfy, satisfying, satisfied, dissatisfied, satisfactory, unsatisfactory, satisfactorily*, etc. In each case note whether the word is a noun, verb, adjective, or adverb.

3   Give out sets of the cards to the students (approximately 20 each). Either in small groups or as a whole class, students make 'domino chains' or steps, by taking turns to place cards on the table, either at the beginning or the end of the chain. Thus a 'word step' might look like this:

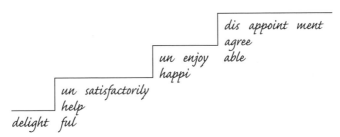

Students are allowed to modify the word part on their card (for example, *–tion* can be used as *–ation, happy* can be changed to *happi*) but the student must identify the alteration (and can re-write it on a blank card). When the chain breaks down, a new one can be started.

Variation

Rather than build a chain, students make as many words as possible from the set of 20 cards, writing them down as they make them. If you want to have a competitive element, you can make sure that each team has an identical set of cards, and the winner is the team that makes the most words.

Follow-up

Students use the words they have made in a written text or spoken dialogue.

3.5 Job cards

Level All levels

Time 15–30 minutes per activity

Aims LANGUAGE Describing job routines, qualities and skills; question forms.

OTHER To practise jobs vocabulary of particular specialisms.

Sample topic Tourism and travel

Transfer Activity can be transferred to any specialism.

Materials Individual job cards (cut up); bingo cards (for 'Description bingo')— one per student.

Preparation

Make cards for 20 jobs that occur in your specialism—or related sectors. 20 may seem high for some professions, but it can usually be achieved if you include people like cleaners, and jobs with an indirect connection.

For 'Description bingo', you will also need to prepare bingo cards, as indicated in 'Procedure'.

Individual job cards (for Tourism)

Pilot	Receptionist	Hotel Manager	Baggage Handler
Tour Guide	Waiter	Airline Check-in Clerk	Hotel Night Manager
Flight Attendant	Resort Rep	Cleaner	Ticket Collector
Tourist Information Officer	Chef	Zoo-keeper	Ski Instructor
Travel Agent	Porter	Tour Operator	Children's Activity Organizer

Photocopiable © Oxford University Press

Description bingo

Student A

Hotel Night Manager	Cleaner	Tour Guide	Tour Operator
Tourist Information Officer	Resort Rep	Receptionist	Zoo-keeper

Student B

Hotel Manager	Ski Instructor	Flight Attendant	Tour Guide
Chef	Baggage Handler	Tour Operator	Porter

Student C

Waiter	Children's Activity Organizer	Resort Rep	Baggage Handler
Tourist Information Officer	Porter	Airline Check-in Clerk	Zoo-keeper

Student D

Ticket Collector	Children's Activity Organizer	Hotel Night Manager	Pilot
Flight Attendant	Receptionist	Hotel Manager	Cleaner

Photocopiable © Oxford University Press

Procedure

Below are four activities using the cards.

1 Put students in groups of three or four, so that each player has a different bingo card.

2 Make sure the students understand the words on their card.

3 Students shuffle the individual cards and place them face down, in a pile.

4 The first player takes the top individual card and must give sentences about the job on the card, without saying the word.

Example
- He/she works in/at a _____ (place).
- He/she works in the _____ (industry sector).
- He/she _____ (a skill or routine).

5 The other players guess the word, the first player giving extra sentences if necessary.

6 When the group has guessed the word correctly, those players who have the word on their Bingo card cross it out.

7 The second player then takes the next individual card and gives a definition, and so on.

8 The first player to cross out all his or her words is the winner.

Who am I?

1 Get students to take one of the individual cards and without looking at it, stick it or clip it to their back (another student can help).

2 The students go round the class asking each other a yes/no question (one question per student) and answering similar questions (for example, Do I work at the airport? Do I have to be willing to work long hours?) until they can identify the job on their back.

3 If they finish early, students take another card and repeat the activity until everyone has found out their first job.

Odd one out

1 Get students to work in groups. They take turns to choose four of the individual cards, one of which should be an 'odd one out', for example, waiter, pilot, flight attendant, ski instructor (pilot is the odd one out because he or she does not usually talk face to face with tourists—but there could be other reasons!).

2 The other students try to guess which one is the odd one out and why.

Variation

You can substitute any groups of words related to the specialism instead of jobs—for example, equipment that is used, places where they work.

Follow-up

Other traditional games can be played as a follow-up—for example, 'What's my line?', 'Twenty questions' or 'Just a minute'.

3.6 The tool-box

Level Pre-intermediate to advanced

Time 40–50 minutes

Aims LANGUAGE Describing importance and necessity.

OTHER To practise vocabulary of equipment for different specialisms, and the lexical chunks in describing their use and importance; to practise speaking skills to explain use of equipment and justify its importance.

Sample topic General

Transfer Activity can be used with any specialism. While it clearly suits the Construction and building trades you can take a broad view of what can go in the tool-box, for example, Medical profession—medical equipment.

Materials Realia or pictures of a range of tools and items that might be found in a tool-box (hammer, screwdriver, etc.).

Procedure

1 Draw (or show) a picture of a tool-box. Explain that it belongs to the caretaker of the building where they work or where you are holding the class.

2 Ask students to say what they think is in the tool-box. Brainstorm and write some items on the board (for example, hammer, spanner, etc.). You can include some light-hearted ones if you want (for example, sandwiches, newspaper) and also some that would definitely *not* be found in a tool-box (for example, ladder). You can avoid naming the items by having pictures or realia, with the words written on them. If you are teaching construction workers, you can teach and practise this vocabulary. If not, it's unnecessary.

3 When you have about six items, get students in pairs to rank them in order of importance.

4 Present phrases for describing use and importance:

Examples • It's important because …
• He/she needs it for …
• It's necessary in order to …
• It can be used for …
• Without x, he/she won't be able to …

5 Get students to compare their orders and try to come up with a consensus order.

6   Get students in whole class to think about six items they would put in a 'tool-box' for their own specialism. For specialisms that do not have special equipment, students can include particular skills (for example, ability to speak another language). They do not need to rank them in order.

7   Get the students to vote on the *least* important item. Count the votes and choose the two items that got the least votes.

8   Nominate two pairs of students. Pair A have to argue why one of the least important items should be included. Pair B have to argue for the other. The rest of the class can prepare questions to ask about the two items.

9   Hold the debate—two minutes presentation by each pair and then two minutes for questions. The class then vote for which of the two items to keep.

10   Repeat the process with the remaining five items and so on until there is only one item left in the tool-box. Nominate different pairs of students each time.

Variation 1

For elementary students, or for students for whom fluency is not a particular need, stop after step 5.

Variation 2

A version of the ELT classic, 'The gift game'. Instead of ranking and voting on the items in the tool-box, the students have to match them to people who could be given them as a present. Students are given a list of people (for example, a recently-qualified plumber, your boss at work, your brother who hates DIY, etc.) and take turns to justify why the 'gift' is perfect for a particular person—the other students then decide whether to accept the match or not.

Follow-up

Get the students to write up a detailed inventory of the tool-box, together with a description of the use and importance of each item.

3.7 Genre switch

Level Pre-intermediate to advanced

Time 50–60 minutes

Aims To identify the lexical features of different registers and genres.

Sample topic Administration and office work

Transfer Activity can be transferred to any specialism, but you may need to emphasize written or spoken registers/genres depending on the particular features of your specialism.

Materials Photocopies of Worksheet 3.7—one per student; photocopies of two prepared texts—one per student.

Preparation

1 Make enough photocopies of Worksheet 3.7 to give one to each student.

2 Establish the main genre types used in texts in your specialism and write two texts relevant to the specialism you are teaching. There are two ways of approaching this:

Examples a keep the two texts authentic
The announcement of the appointment of a new CEO: the first text can be the official announcement issued by the Board of Directors (We are pleased to announce the appointment of … etc.); the second can be a colleague to colleague email (By the way have you heard that they've given the CEO job to … etc.).

b two texts where the genre has been completely switched
A scientific report written in the style of a school-report, or a letter to the bank asking for a loan written in the style of a love letter.

Procedure

1 Set the scene: an employee working in a large office has an urgent email to send, but unfortunately her computer has broken down.

2 Give out Worksheet 3.7 and get students to match the four statements in column A to the situations in column B.

3 In pairs, get the students to analyze the different features:
   • Which ones are spoken and which are written?
   • What is the relationship between the speaker/writer and the listener/reader?
   • How is the vocabulary different in the various statements and utterances in column A?

Answer: The word *use* remains consistent (although it is a noun rather than a verb in statement 4), but the enabling language changes according to the different register (formal/informal, spoken/written).

Worksheet 3.7

A	B
1 Sorry, but I need to use your computer.	a Entry in staff handbook.
2 Due to a technical fault in the HR Department, we would appreciate the opportunity to use your computer on Thursday between the hours of 14.00 and 16.00.	b Manager to employee.
3 Is it all right if I use your computer this afternoon?	c Memo from one department to another.
4 Access to and use of IT facilities by different departments may be required from time to time. This should be confirmed by management.	d Colleague to colleague.

Photocopiable © Oxford University Press

4 Having established the features of contrasting registers used to express the same function, now develop this into looking at contrasting genres by introducing the two texts you have prepared. In pairs, get students to analyze the lexical differences between the two contrasting texts.

5 In pairs, each student writes a text to a colleague (for example, email asking them to do a particular specialism-related task).

6 The texts are swapped between partners and changed into a contrasting genre—for example, line manager to employee (type 'A'), or a completely different genre, such as a love letter, business letter, crime novel, advertisement, etc. (type 'B').

Variation

Get students to brainstorm as many different genres as they can. Select any one of these at random to write a text for step 6. At the end the author writes the name of a different genre and exchanges it with a partner, who has to transform the text into the named genre.

Follow-up

Identify the genre and register of any other texts that you have used—or that are used in the future. Have a regular 'genre-switching' lesson or assignment where the texts are transformed into a contrasting genre.

3.8 Corpora

Level Intermediate to advanced

Time 30 minutes for Session 1, 50–60 minutes for Session 2

Aims LANGUAGE General lexical work, with particular emphasis on comprehension, context, deducing meaning, and collocation.

OTHER To introduce students to using reference and research sources for vocabulary work—such as corpora, dictionaries, Internet search engines, and subject reference books; to present ways in which corpora can be exploited by the learners.

Sample topic Medicine and healthcare

Transfer Activity can be transferred to any specialism, but the direct use of corpora will be most useful in academic subjects (especially EAP), and Information Technology (where the deeper exploration of the computer science behind corpora can combine subject-related and language-related work).

Materials Computers with access to online corpora and search engines; English–English dictionaries (and possibly bilingual as well); subject reference books and coursebooks (ideally in English); photocopies of concordance—one per student.

Preparation

1 Make certain you are familiar with how corpora (and concordance lists) work, by looking at some of the examples given.

2 Gather the materials as described above. Set up the computers with downloaded corpora, such as British National Corpus – Variations in English Words and Phrases (www.view.byu.edu).

Note check http://devoted.to/corpora for latest available corpora, including free online access.

3 Make concordance worksheets for your specialism as described in Session 2, Steps 2 to 5.

Procedure

Session 1

1 On the board write a technical word or phrase from the specialism, for example, *heart-rate, monitor*, or *haemophilia*.

2 Ask the students: *What do you understand by the term? What type of text would it appear in? What words might surround it? Can you write a sentence with it?* Do not confirm or reject anything at this step.

3 Divide the class into four groups, and give one of the following resources to each group:

A Computer with corpora websites
B Dictionaries (English-English, and possibly bilingual as well)
C Computer with Internet search engine
D Subject reference books, preferably in English.

4 Ask the students to research the word or phrase, and report on how useful their resource is for the following criteria:
- helping with the meaning of the word or phrase
- provision of a context
- association with grammatical patterns (and parts of speech)
- frequency of use
- register of use (for example, spoken/written, formal/informal)
- collocations (words that are usually associated with it)
- ways of finding out more about the subject of the word or phrase
- any other advantages (for example, how accessible and easy to use is the resource?).

You may want to set this as an out-of-class assignment to be reported on in the next session. If you do the activity in class, you may want to let the groups look at different resources, as some will finish their research sooner.

Session 2

1 Report back on what the students found out in their research. Discuss the relative advantages of the four resources for improving vocabulary understanding and use. The basic conclusions will probably be something like this:

A **Corpora**—gives authentic examples and data on frequency of use, allows selection of specific uses (for example, in different registers), analyzes grammatical patterns associated with the word or phrase, particularly good on providing examples of collocation.

B **English–English dictionary**—gives basic information (meaning, pronunciation, example sentences, related words) and is easy to use.

C **Search engine**—gives example sentences, but most significant is that it gives access to a vast range of information sources (and authentic texts).

D **Subject reference books**—gives examples of use and explains meaning, and is located in the overall structure of the specialism.

2 Give out Worksheet 3.8a for *monitor* (or another keyword from your specialism). Get students to find examples of:
- use as noun/use as verb
- words that appear before and after the keyword (i.e. possible collocations)
- other specialist words that appear in the extracts
- other features that might be associated with the keyword (for example, prepositions used with it, whether it can ever be a proper noun with capital letter, and so on).

3 Give out Worksheet 3.8b, this time with the target word gapped out. You can either have the same word (for example, *pulse*), or a pair of associated words (for example, *heart* and *pulse*, or *heart* and *blood*) and jumble the lines. Students have to deduce the missing word, and then note aspects about it such as they looked at in step 2. They can also attempt to extend the sentence extracts (before and after).

4   Now demonstrate how the corpus can be used for collocations. Use an example of a keyword (*heart*)—get students to predict the most frequent collocations with the keyword. Show how the computer lists collocations and their frequency. You can either do this 'live' on screen, if you are in a computer lab, or by means of copied worksheets.

5   Give out a further list of collocations in context with one of the keywords of each collocation gapped (either the bold or the italic in the sample texts). See if the students can guess the words. This can be done as an information gap, with A (bold) checking their answers with B (italic). If the students are in a computer lab, they can use the corpus/concordance to help them. Sample texts are given in Worksheet 3.8c.

Note: It should not be necessary to explain how the 'significance' is calculated: it is sufficient just to show the relative frequency of the collocations.

Worksheet 3.8a

Concordance examples for *monitor*
(selected on 'academic' and 'medicine')

proof of achievements and which sought to **monitor** progress systematically. Most adverse
of assessment which could **monitor** the development of all children for
each of the group sessions to **monitor** their drinking levels. Although it may
public confidence in the independent judicial **monitor**. For the Labour Party, Mr Kaufman said
patients do not need to home **monitor** every day when their diabetes is
or inject themselves with insulin, **monitor** their blood glucose levels, to be careful of
reasons for selecting the BAC1-11 Pitch **Monitor** Unit were as follows. The unit had
medical publisher had enabled us to **monitor** early attempts to move from a traditional print-based
years have enabled us to **monitor** the single-cell correlates of behavioural activity in
and the visual cortex acting as the TV **monitor**. Activity in the visual cortex will therefore

---

Variation 1

For more vocational specialisms, the corpora will probably only be accessed by the teacher in order to ensure the use of authentic language examples, and set activities of the type suggested in Session 2, steps 3 and 5. In this case, the whole of Session 1 and the reporting back step of Session 2 can be omitted.

Variation 2

For students who are academically-minded and who need to work with data at a high level, you can get them to create their own corpus for their specialism. This can be done by analyzing the texts in 1.6, 'Authentic materials bank' and 3.2, 'Word stew'.

Worksheet 3.8b

Concordance samples for *heart* and *pulse* (selected on 'spoken' and 'medicine')

consequences, so let's try to get to the _____	of it tonight, one hundred women are prepared
is concussed. Their breathing will become shallow and the _____	rapid and weak, where's your casualty
me with my finger on that _____	to have made that point to the
compared to other people who need a _____	transplant or a kidney transplant
you got a tone telephone or a _____	telephone? It's probably a switch
legs at all, we've found a _____	in his left leg, but we can't find one
between starting smoking and developing lung cancer or _____	disease or developing
you know that video off by _____	, you should do so when you play safe
very tempting when you have set your _____	on something like that. And very tempting
and so on, one took my temperature and felt my _____	and that, this and that, he said
sixty to eighty, you can feel it at _____	point can't you here, here, we'll
talk by Doctor Tom for the British _____	Foundation. Sounds good. Folk Hall,
become unconscious, they stop breathing, their _____	stops, then everything else has to
will produce an identifiable electrical _____	and I can look at that and learn

Variation 3

If you want to avoid corpora altogether, an alternative way of using authentic texts to practise deducing meaning from context is to use missing word headlines. Get headlines or other extracts from specialist journals and newsletters. Gap out keywords and get students in pairs to predict the missing word(s) by deducing from context. Students can also gap out their own words from the headlines and test each other. Extend further by writing the story that follows, either the whole story by one student or pair, or passing the story round the class with each person/pair adding a section.

Example   *Collocation sampler screen for heart*

The exact appearance will depend on which of the corpora you use, but you should get something like this:

heart	**significance**
attack	22.2
disease	20.9
problems	11.5
rate	10.4
throb	8.5

failure	8.4
beat	8.1
shaped	7.7
surgery	7.4
condition	7.1

Follow-up

Students can get further practice at using corpora by making their own concordance gap-fills and collocation lists, which they then set for each other to complete.

Comments

By their very nature, corpora are changing and developing all the time. One of the best websites to access corpora is David Lee's frequently updated corpus website at http://devoted.to/corpora. The idea of corpora can sometimes seem daunting to learner and teacher alike, but it shouldn't be forgotten that we have already suggested the use of non-computer based corpora in the form of activities such as the 1.6, 'Authentic Materials Bank' and 3.2, 'Word stew'.

Acknowledgements

The Concordance samples are taken from www.byu.edu

Worksheet 3.8c

Sample collocation texts

A Tourism

San Francisco is a wonderful *city*. It offers everything for the tourist: from beautiful *parks* and spectacular *views* to exciting *night-life*, delicious *food* and fine *dining* in some of the many varied and interesting restaurants. There is an efficient *transport system* to take you around: you can ride the historic *cable-cars* over the dramatic *hills* or travel by ferry to the famous *attraction* of Alcatraz. And of course there is the special *hospitality* of Californians to look after you.

B Machine trades

Cleaning a *battery*:

Disconnect negative (black) *cable* from battery.

Disconnect positive (red) *cable*.

Unscrew *wing-nuts*.

Remove *battery*.

Clean *battery* with weak baking soda solution.

Rinse all *parts* with cold water.

Install *battery*.

Replace *wing-nuts*.

Connect positive *cable*.

Connect negative *cable*.

C Nursing

Patient care plan—check-list

Check *breathing* ___

Check *pulse rate* ___

Check *heart rate* ___

Take blood pressure *reading* ___

Monitor oxygen *levels* ___

Ensure *patient* is alert ___

Introduce *oral fluids* ___

Administer prescribed *drugs* ___

Monitor *effect* of drugs ___

Observe *wound site* for bleeding ___

Inform *medical staff* of any change ___

Photocopiable © Oxford University Press

4

Processes, procedures, and operating systems

At first glance it might be thought that this chapter relates mainly to manufacturing and scientific specialisms—the production line, the carefully staged experiment, the people with white coats and clipboards. But it is not only the technical and mechanical specialisms that have processes, procedures, and operating systems: all students will need to know how things work in their specialism. In nursing this could be the procedure for admitting a patient or for preparing for an operation. In hotel management it could be the food and beverage cycle dealing with the ordering, preparation, and delivery of catering services. In finance it could be the procedure for preparing budgets, financial reports, and audits.

There are a number of language areas that recur in this topic—sequencers, the present simple passive, describing function and purpose, conditionals—and the first group of activities (4.1, 'Get in order' to 4.5, 'Building a bridge') will use these language areas when analyzing various processes, procedures and systems. In later activities (4.6, 'Living without it' to 4.9, 'Keeping to schedule') students will be taking a more productive approach: designing, re-designing and improving systems related to their specialism.

The final activity (4.10, 'Designing a flying machine') is a longer activity, over two sessions, and brings together many of the themes and ideas explored in earlier activities. It is a much freer activity and is as much about team-building and exploring group dynamics (which is of course a system in its own right) as it is about process and procedure.

4.1 Get in order

Level Pre-intermediate to advanced

Time 10–15 minutes (warmer), 40–50 minutes (main activity)

Aims LANGUAGE Sequencers; verb forms: imperative and present simple passive.

OTHER To establish the concepts of process and procedure.

Sample topic General

Materials Texts describing the stages of three different processes—one per student—use examples or produce your own, but try not to use processes that come directly from the specialism, as students will be producing these in step 4.

Preparation

Copy and cut up the three texts, with each stage of the process on a separate piece of paper. For larger classes you will need more than one copy of each text.

Example processes

(If these processes are used, some pre-teaching of lexis may be necessary.)

A Making olive oil

Firstly, the olives are harvested at the end of autumn.

1 A large net is spread under the olive tree in order to catch the olives when the tree is shaken.

2 Then the olives are collected and put into large baskets.

3 After collecting the olives, they are taken to an olive press.

4 Before pressing the olives it is important to make sure that the olives are washed and leaves have been removed.

5 The olives are first of all pressed in the 'preparatory' press, which is used to extract the first oil and which is sold as 'virgin olive oil'.

6 Then they are pressed in the 'final' press, in order to get more oil.

7 The oil from the final pressing is refined and blended, and sold as 'blended olive oil'.

Photocopiable © Oxford University Press

Stage 4 can be broken into two stages if you need more stages to allow every student to have one.

B Changing a tyre

1 First of all, take out the spare wheel and tools from the boot of the car, and check that the tyre is inflated.

2 Remove the wheel cover.

3 Then, using the wheel brace, loosen the nuts on the wheel you are changing by half a turn.

4 Use the jack to raise the wheel, making sure that you place the jack in the correct lifting point on the car.

5 When the wheel is clear of the ground, unscrew the nuts and remove them.

6 Remove the damaged wheel.

7 Next, fit the spare wheel and fit the wheel nuts until finger-tight.

8 Using the jack, lower the car until the wheel just touches the ground.

9 Use the wheel brace to tighten the wheel nuts.

10 Finally remove the jack and check the nuts are fully tight.

Photocopiable © Oxford University Press

C Making a sale

1 Start by raising client awareness—make sure they are already thinking about your products and services even before you talk to them.

2 On first meeting it is important to create a good relationship with the client.

3 As soon as possible find out what your client is interested in.

4 When you know what they are generally interested in, show the client a range of products and services.

5 Give details of the products and services you are showing, and make recommendations.

6 Having done this, it is important to give the client time to think.

7 Follow-up by asking if the client has any further questions.

8 After allowing sufficient time, try to close the sale—but don't be too pushy: the client may need more time.

Photocopiable © Oxford University Press

Procedure

Warmer

1 Ask students to think of a process or procedure that they do in their daily work or routine—something that involves a series of steps or stages and which they do regularly.

2 Demonstrate a mime of your own process, for example, making a cake, or getting into a car and driving off.

3 Nominate one of the students to mime the process they have thought of in front of the class.

4 When another student thinks they know what the process is, they join in the mime, taking over one of the stages.

Main activity

1 Give each student a different stage in one of the processes (for example, making olive oil). The students mingle and get themselves in the correct order, and then read out the stages to check. With larger classes it may be easier to do it sitting in groups.

2 In pairs or groups the students are given jumbled up stages of the two other processes. They must separate the two processes, and then put the stages in order. At the end they can compare with another group to check.

3 Focus on all three processes and identify the key language (sequencers, present simple passive, and imperatives).

4 Finally students produce their own processes (two if possible) from their specialism, and jumble them up for other groups to sort out.

Variation 1

If you feel that drama techniques are not appropriate for your group, leave out the warmer.

Variation 2

For elementary students reduce the number of processes (and simplify language where possible). Pictures also may help.

Variation 3

To add an extra element, get the students to remove one vital stage from their processes, and then see if the other groups can work out what is missing.

Follow-up

Convert the process description to a report, following the report-writing conventions of the specialism. This will also involve using past simple forms.

4.2 What does it do?

Level Pre-intermediate to advanced

Time 30–40 minutes

Aims LANGUAGE Describing purpose and function; verbs associated with control devices.

OTHER To explain the function of equipment and simple processes.

Sample topic General

Transfer Activity can be used with any specialism. It is most relevant to more technical specialisms, but most people use mobile phones in some capacity.

Materials Any remote control devices and mobile phones you have available (i.e. devices with buttons).

Preparation

Draw a diagram of a 'Universal remote control' (for example, for television and video) on the board. See example.

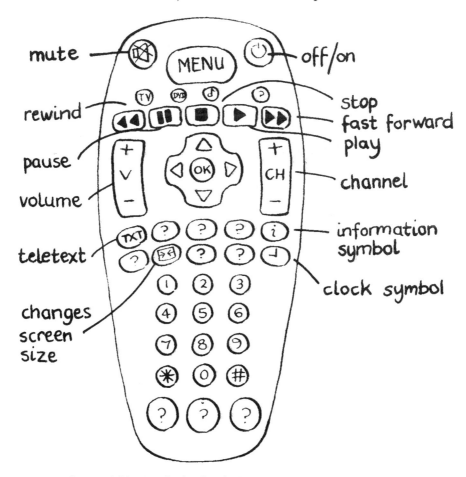

Procedure

1 Identify some of the buttons on your 'universal remote control' with standard symbols (for example, symbols for *play, fast forward, stop*, etc.). Make sure some of the buttons are left blank as these will be needed in step 5.

2 Identify the function of the keys you have labelled with a symbol, by getting the students to write a simple function/process sentence, for example, *It turns the power off. It fast forwards.* Report back.

3 Put students in groups of two or three. Give each group a remote control device. Also ask them to take out their mobile phones, if they have them. In groups, students identify the different functions of the different keys.

4 In groups, get students to think about remote devices of the future and the functions they might perform: What will they be able to do and control? What would the students like them to do and control? Encourage fantasy and wackiness and maybe give some examples such as: automatically feed the cat or drive the car for you.

5 When the groups have agreed on two or three new functions, representatives from each group should take turns to come to the board and label one of the spare buttons on the 'universal remote control' with an appropriate symbol or letter for one of the new functions. The other students try to guess what the button does.

Variation 1

For elementary students you may want to stop the activity after step 3.

Variation 2

Make the suggested new functions in steps 4 and 5 specific to the students' jobs and daily tasks.

Follow-up

Write an instruction sheet on 'How to use the universal remote control'. The activity could also link up with 4.10, 'Designing a flying machine'.

4.3 Procedures brainstorm

Level Elementary to advanced

Time 15–20 minutes

Aims LANGUAGE Sequencers; present simple for procedure/routine.

OTHER To discuss procedures; to improve fluency by working within set time limits.

Sample topic General

Materials Pieces of paper with a different procedure written on each—one per group.

Preparation

Think of a range of procedures that are either of universal relevance or particularly relevant to the specialism you are teaching.

Example
- Airport arrival (check-in, passport control, etc.)
- Registration at a conference
- Enrolment on a school or college course
- Buying a house or flat
- Organizing an 'information seminar' or promotional event
- Driving a car (from getting in to driving off)
- Any of the procedures mentioned in previous activities in this chapter.

Procedure

1 Divide the class into groups of two or three.

2 Give each group the title of a procedure.

3 Each group has five minutes to discuss and write down the stages of the procedure they have been given. Be strict on the time!

4 The procedures are passed to the group on the left, with each group given two minutes to add, modify, and refine before passing it on again. You should be available to provide key vocabulary as needed.

5 The activity ends when the procedures have been all round the circle and are back with their original authors.

Follow-up

Write up the procedures in their final version in the form of an operator's or instructor's manual.

Comments

Passing/modifying activities like this can be done with other text types, not just procedures.

4.4 Circulation and flow

Level Intermediate to advanced

Time 30–40 minutes

Aims LANGUAGE Vocabulary related to circulation—for example, *pump,
pressure*; present simple; the passive; defining and non-
defining relative clauses.

OTHER To practise language of describing technical processes,
in particular systems involving circulation and flow; to
identify language similarities between two different
processes from two different specialisms.

Sample topic Medicine and health care; Engineering

Transfer The activity can be transferred to any specialism where a technical
approach is required.

Materials Diagrams of (a) human circulation system, and (b) domestic central
heating system.

Preparation

Copy the text with the descriptions of the two processes mixed up.
The words 'blood' and 'water' have been removed to make it more
challenging. But if you want to make it easier, you can keep them in.
Note also that one of the subsidiary aims of the activity is to get
students to distinguish the technical language they need from other
technical terms they can discard—hence the two contrasting
specialisms used here.

Jumbled text (blood circulation and central heating systems)

The system consists of a boiler, a network of pipes, a feed, an
expansion tank, radiators, and a hot _____ storage system.
_____ **is pumped round the system by** electrical pumps.
The heart pumps _____ in a one-way circuit through
vessels, which are like small pipes. _____ **is circulated
through** a heat exchanger. There are in fact **two main circuits**.
One loop **passes through** the inside of the storage cylinder in a
coil arrangement. The pulmonary lung circuit **carries** _____
from the right side of the heart to the lungs to pick up oxygen. **It
then returns** oxygen-rich _____ to the left side of the heart.
Heat **is then transferred to** the surrounding _____, which
can **be drawn off** at various points in the system when required.
The other circuit **carries** oxygen-rich _____ from the left
side of the heart to the rest of the body. It also **returns** oxygen-
poor _____ to the right side of the heart. Another circuit
passes to the radiators, **which provide** room heating.

Photocopiable © Oxford University Press

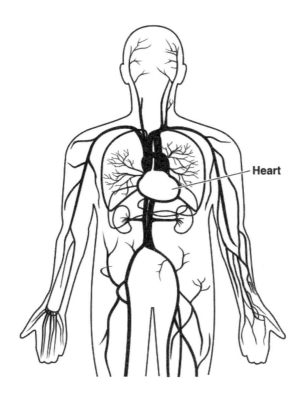

Heart

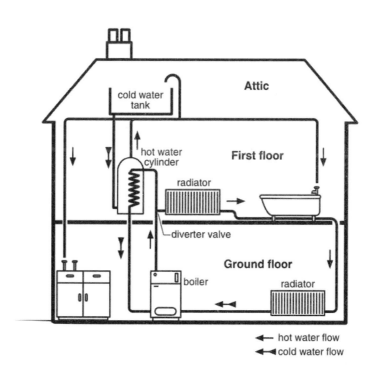

Procedure

1 Pre-teach some of the important vocabulary by referring to the diagrams.

2 In pairs, get students to unjumble the text—separating out the blood circulation and central heating parts.

3 Identify similar language—nouns, verbs, semi-technical words, lexical phrases for describing technical systems (some suggestions are highlighted in the text above), as well as grammar areas such as the present simple, the passive, and defining and non-defining relative clauses.

4 Label the diagrams and add numbers to refer to the processes described in the text. Compare similarities and differences.

Variation

Give students the 'wrong' diagram to label—i.e. students use the blood circulation text to label the central heating system (and *vice versa*). This adds an element of fun, at the same time as reinforcing the point about similarities and differences.

Follow-up

Describe other systems from the specialism and relate descriptions to labelled diagrams.

Comments

For other specialisms the activity may still be worth doing as it is—as it demonstrates how language forms and styles often operate across disciplines—but you may prefer to substitute with an alternative pair of related but different processes. For example, in the hospitality industry you could compare the food and beverage cycle in a big hotel restaurant, with the housekeeping and maintenance cycle in a hotel. Other examples could be: the traffic flow system, the internal postal system of a large company or institution, organizing and running an international meeting.

4.5 Building a bridge

Level Pre-intermediate to advanced

Time 40–50 minutes

Aims LANGUAGE Describing purpose; comparatives.

      OTHER   To examine how different systems, processes and procedures are used to achieve similar results.

Sample topic Engineering; Construction and building trades

Transfer Activity can be transferred to any specialism. For students of Engineering or Science, spend longer on the technical bridge stage. For non-science students, spend longer on the final steps, using ideas suggested in step 5.

Materials Drawings or pictures of six bridge types (*arch, beam, lifting, cantilever, suspension, cable-stayed*).

Preparation

Research suitable material for your specialism—you need something like the bridges example, where there is a basic common aim (for example, with bridges it's getting across a river, a valley, or some other obstacle) and a variety of systems or processes to achieve it.

Procedure

1 Introduce the concept of similar processes used to achieve similar aims by discussing in open class different ways of cooking: gas, electricity, fire, etc. All are ways of cooking food, but why are different ones used, and what are they each best for?

2 Do a similar activity in pairs or groups with another example, not from the students' own specialism, for example, the different ways of easing pain— drugs, massage, acupuncture, tea and sympathy.

3 Draw, or provide pictures of, the six bridge types and ask students to try to think of a famous example of each or one from their local area.

4 Get the students to discuss in pairs or groups the advantages of each type of bridge and why it is used in the particular examples they have found. The chart below may help you for reference.

5 The class have now had three different examples of different systems or processes to achieve a common generic aim. They should now be asked to apply the same thinking to their own specialism. Here are some suggestions:
- Business and commerce—ways of investing sums of money.
- Tourism—different ways of travelling to holiday resorts; different types of accommodation.
- Construction and building trades—different types of wall.
- Medicine and health care—different methods of emergency or first aid care.
- Academic—different ways of revising for examinations.
- Administration and office work—different ways of communicating (i.e. phone, email, etc.).

Type	Illustration	Example	Advantages
Arch		London Bridge	Strong because weight is pushed outwards to the abutments rather than downwards
Beam		most city road bridges	Good for carrying a heavy load over a short distance
Lifting		Tower Bridge	Hydraulic power lifts a section of the bridge up to allow tall ships etc. to pass underneath
Cantilever		Forth Railway Bridge, Scotland	Good for carrying a heavy load over a greater distance. The load is balanced on two piers.
Suspension		Golden Gate Bridge, San Francisco	Spans hang on steel wires from a cable between two tall towers. Good for spanning wide expanses of water.
Cable-stayed		QE2 Bridge, Dartford	Similar to a suspension bridge but the cables are in fixed positions. Also good for spanning wide expanses of water.

6   In groups, the students draw up a list of the advantages of each process, procedure, or method. Then compare with other groups to reach a class consensus.

Variation

Instead of making steps 2–5 sequential, divide the class into three groups and give each group one of the topics to work on: A—different ways of easing pain, B—bridges, C—their own specialism. This will allow you to give more challenging topics to stronger students. At the end have a plenary discussion or presentation stage on the three topics.

Follow-up

1 Prepare a written report or instruction leaflet on the advantages and disadvantages of the different processes and systems.

2 Write out step-by-step descriptions of how each of their chosen processes or systems is built or achieved.

4.6 Living without it

Level	Elementary to advanced
Time	15–20 minutes
Aims	LANGUAGE Describing function and purpose.
	OTHER To analyze the function of a piece of equipment and the process or procedure by which it is used.
Sample topic	Construction and building trades
Transfer	Activity can be transferred to any specialism which uses equipment.

Procedure

1 Ask students what they think the most important piece of equipment for a teacher is. Choose two of their ideas that you are in rough agreement with—one might be obvious (for example, cassette machine/CD player), one less so (for example, your voice). Discuss in class how you would cope without them: what alternative systems and procedures would you adopt? (For example, for cassette machine—read scripts out aloud; for voice—use mime, get a student to be your voice.)

2 Get students to think of a really important piece of equipment in their specialism, for example, 'ladder' for construction workers.

3 Tell the students to imagine that the piece of equipment doesn't exist anymore. In pairs, they should design an alternative piece of equipment or procedure. For construction workers, alternatives to a ladder might be standing on a chair or your colleague's shoulders (not safe), or building a scaffold tower (much safer), or employing extra tall people!

In every case, they can discuss what they would do if 'voice' was the missing piece of equipment. This will have the effect of not only getting them to think about new communication procedures and processes in general, but also identify the areas where spoken English is needed in their specialism.

4 Students compare their alternatives with each other. You can award a prize for the best and for the most bizarre/ingenious alternatives. With higher level groups you might want to discuss whether the alternatives have made them think more about the equipment they use—for example, the danger of over-reliance on one thing, and whether in some cases the alternative might be an improvement.

Variation 1

Instead of discussing the important pieces of equipment in open class, get students to keep it secret. Other students then have to guess what the alternative is replacing.

Variation 2

Extend the activity by getting the students to replace *every* piece of equipment they use—for example, creating an office or workshop where there is no technical equipment, or even any electricity.

Comments

The activity can lead into 4.10, 'Designing a flying machine'.

4.7 Routed calls

Level Intermediate to advanced

Time 50–60 minutes

Aims LANGUAGE Infinitive of purpose; *if* clauses/conditionals; vocabulary of phones and mobile phone services.

OTHER To practise telephone service procedures through analysis of call-routing systems.

Sample topic Phone-based services

Transfer Activity is most relevant to service-based specialisms, but call-routing is something all people will probably encounter at some time.

Materials Either a tape recording of the suggested mobile phone call routing script (or your own one if you prefer), or a printed version (ideally on an overhead transparency or Powerpoint slide).

Preparation

Prepare the tape recording or script. If, as suggested, you are going to elicit the stages of the route map stage by stage, then make sure you can reveal the script easily (for example, by covering relevant parts of an overhead transparency).

Procedure

1 Ask students if they have ever called an automated phone-line. What are their experiences—good and bad? Discuss the advantages and disadvantages of such systems both from the user/customer side and the company/service side.

2 Explain that they are going to hear (or read) the 'route map' of a mobile phone company's automated line. Elicit the services they would expect to hear on the main menu.

3 Play the tape (or read the tapescript) to check.

4 Elicit the options they would expect for each of the four services offered on the main menu. Again play the tape or read the tapescript of the second stage menus to check.

Mobile phone route map

Main menu

- Hello, you're through to Phoneworld. To help us deal with your enquiry, please choose one of the following options:
- To top up, press 1.
- If you're having problems with your phone, or if it has been lost, stolen, or damaged, press 2.
- To buy an extra service or upgrade your phone, or to make changes to your tariff, press 3.
- To find out your current credit balance, press 4.

Second stage menus

1
- To top up using a credit card or debit card, press 1.
- To use a Phoneworld swipe card, press 2.
- To use a pre-paid voucher, press 3.
- To set up a Direct Debit, press 4.

2
- If your phone's been lost or stolen, press 1.
- If you're having problems making or receiving calls, or with text or voice messaging, press 2.
- For help with features like video email or photo-messaging, press 3.

3
- For changes to your tariff, press 1.
- For information on upgrading your phone, press 2.
- For information on using your phone abroad, press 3.

Third stage menu
(from Second stage menu, option 3.3)

- To find out about using your phone abroad, press 1.
- To find out about calling another country from your country, press 2.

Fourth stage menu
(from Third stage menu, option 1)

- To find out the cost of calling your country from abroad, text the word 'from' plus the country you'd like to call from, to 452.
- To speak to someone about calling from abroad, press 2.

5 Before you play or read the third stage of the route map, set the situation of someone phoning because they want to know if they can use their 'pay-as-you-go' phone when they are abroad. Ask which buttons they should have pressed in the main menu and the second stage menu.

6 Play the third stage menu and elicit which button to press (the answer is 1).

7 Do the same with the next and final stage (the answer is 2).

8 Put the students into groups of three or four. Tell them they are going to write the route map and full menu options for an automated phone line to their company or place of work or study. Ask the students:

- What are the main services that the company provides?
- What exactly would callers want to know and find out about these services?
- Are there any services that you want to 'sell' to callers? How can you guide callers to these services?
- How can the route map be made as efficient and as friendly as possible, without using a real person until it is absolutely necessary?

Then they should write the route map in detail. They should write the exact words (in order to practise appropriate politeness and register).

9 Each member of the group should then think of two or three enquiries that callers might phone with. The group should test the enquiries on their route map and modify if necessary.

10 Finally, the groups can test their enquiries on the route maps of other groups, and decide whose is the best.

Variation

For more advanced students, all the options from every stage of the mobile phone route map could be cut up and jumbled so that students first have to order them according to which stage of the process they belong to. This can help with discourse analysis and understanding referencing within texts.

Follow-up

1 Role-play the same enquiries but this time the phone is answered by a real person. Analyze how the language is different. You could present this by playing a tape of a non-automated phone enquiry.

2 Discuss not only the language differences, but which system is better—including which system is better for people whose first language is not the same.

4.8 Improving work procedures and time management

Level Pre-intermediate to advanced

Time 30–40 minutes

Aims LANGUAGE Describing job routines and activities (simple present, *I spend (a lot of time) -ing*); *too much/not enough.*

       OTHER To promote discussion of job activities and procedures, including their frustrations and ways of improving time management, delegation, and other related skills.

Sample topic Business and commerce; Administration and office work

Transfer Activity can be transferred to any specialism, but you will need to adapt the verbs that are put on the word cards.

Materials Photocopies of word cards; a piece of paper with four columns headed: 'too much', 'a lot', 'not much', 'not enough'—one per group.

Preparation

Cut up as many sets of the word cards as you need for your class—students will work in groups of 2–3.

Procedure

1 Distribute sets of the word cards to groups of two or three students.

2 Check understanding of the verbs (and any prepositions they use) by asking for collocations. *What can you* check/plan? *Who can you* chat to? *What can you* chat about? etc. Write the collocations on the board.

3 Give out the paper with the four columns ('too much', 'a lot', 'not much', 'not enough'), and ask the students to put the collocated words in one of the four categories, according to the time they spend on the activity.

4 Ask students to look at the words they've put in the 'too much' and 'not enough' columns. How could they improve their daily procedures, their time management, self-discipline, and delegation on those tasks?

Variation

For elementary students reduce the number of word cards used, or provide a list of collocations and activities from the specialism.

Follow-up

1 Get the students to prepare an action plan as a result of their findings in this activity. The plan should be aimed at decreasing those verbs and activities that occur in the 'too much' and 'not enough' columns, and should be revisited after a period of time, to see if there is any improvement.

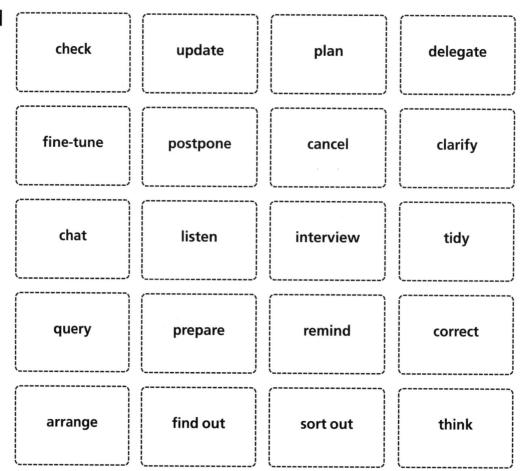

check	update	plan	delegate
fine-tune	postpone	cancel	clarify
chat	listen	interview	tidy
query	prepare	remind	correct
arrange	find out	sort out	think

2 Prepare a work-based questionnaire using the verbs/collocations—i.e. *How much time do you spend -ing?* Give the questionnaire to work colleagues and analyze the results to suggest ways of improving workplace practice.

Acknowledgements

This activity is based on an activity presented by David Grant for Oxford University Press at IATEFL BESIG 2004 (Personalized activities for busy teachers).

4.9 Keeping to schedule

Level Pre-intermediate to advanced

Time 40–50 minutes

Aims LANGUAGE Discussing possibility and probability; suggesting changes; giving opinions, agreeing and disagreeing.

OTHER To look at longer term processes and procedures through 'Programmes of work'; to adapt such programmes according to changing events.

Sample topic Construction and building trade

Transfer Activity can be transferred to any specialism which has long-term processes.

Materials A 'Programme of work' schedule for the specialism you are working with—an example for the building trade is provided.

Preparation

1 Think of a 'Programme of work' schedule that might occur in the specialism you are teaching, and which would take a number of weeks or months to complete—for example, a building project or the launch of a new product or area of activity.

2 Prepare the 'Programme of work' schedule (see example). You can prepare this without expert knowledge, because the activity will go better if there are errors and omissions in it (which the students can correct and discuss).

Example *Programme of work (Construction and building trades)*

Week commencing	18 Apr	25 Apr	2 May	9 May	16 May	23 May
Setting out	MT					
Excavate foundation trenches	WTF					
Lay concrete foundations		MT				
Brickwork to DPC		WTF				
Hardcore concrete to ground floor			MT			
Brickwork to 1st floor			WTF	M		
1st floor joists				TW		
Brickwork to eaves				TF	M	
Roof structure					TWT	
Tile roof					F	M

(Department of Education and Skills, *Skills for Life: Materials for Embedded Learning—Trowel occupations*)

Procedure

1 Give out the 'Programme of work' schedule you have prepared. Check all the vocabulary is understood.

2 In groups, get students to analyse it and revise it if necessary. In particular they should decide:
   • if all the stages are there
   • if they are in the correct order
   • if the time allocated is appropriate.

3 Groups compare their revised Programmes, and make any further changes they think are needed.

4 The activity then becomes a simulation, with groups imagining that the Programme has now started. As time progresses, you should throw in events and problems that may affect the Programme and necessitate changes. Students in their groups have to decide if the event will affect their schedule or not. If it does, they will need to make changes, trying to keep to the final deadline as far as possible.

Here are some suggestions of fairly universal problems that might affect any specialism:

Week 1: terrible weather (storms and rain)
Week 2: transport strike (all public transport stopped for two weeks)
Week 3: serious staff sickness (25% of workforce off sick for a week)
Week 4: public holiday (only a four-day week)
Week 5: new urgent project comes up (original project has to be
             speeded up or reduced)
Week 6: project leader resigns to take a job at a rival company.

5 At the end the groups compare their revised Programmes of work and decide who is delivering the best one.

Variation

For pre-work students step 2 will be tricky, and you will either have to guide students through it carefully (which may be a useful thing to do in its own right) or drop it and go straight to step 4 (ensuring that you have a fairly accurate Programme in the first place). It could also be very useful (especially for pre-work students) for you to talk to a colleague who teaches the subject and who can give you some typical solutions to the problems in step 4. Students can compare their own solutions with the expert.

Follow-up

Get the students to prepare a detailed Programme of work for their own studies, including English language learning.

4.10 Designing a flying machine

Level   Intermediate to advanced

Time   50 minutes for Session 1, 50 minutes for Session 2 (longer if you want students to build the machine).

Aims   LANGUAGE Semi-technical vocabulary: simple equipment and machine parts, verbs of movement; passive/active for processes; present continuous.

OTHER   To get students thinking about design and function; to get students working together on a practical material project that will involve them allocating roles and tasks and deciding on procedures and schedules of work.

Sample topic   General

Transfer   Activity can be used with any specialism which needs to establish and work with clear procedures and processes, and where group dynamics and teamwork are important.

Materials   Session 1—a bicycle (ideally a real one, but if not, a picture of one); photocopies of cartoons A and B. Session 2—none—unless you are going to go ahead with the actual construction!

This is a two-session activity which brings together many of the themes explored in the other activities.

Preparation

Make enough copies of the cartoons for one copy of each per pair of students.

Procedure

Session 1

1   Use the bicycle to teach the language of machines and their operation.

Example   The pedals turn the front cog which is connected by a chain to the rear cog which drives the rear wheel. A system of cogs or gears allows the speed of the machine to be adjusted. The speed of the bicycle is also regulated by the speed of pedalling. When the brake lever is pulled it pulls a wire which is connected to the wheel-braking system. This slows the machine.

2   Get the students to think of other simple machines—for example, a coffee-grinder, a garlic-crusher, a lifting pulley. Get them to describe how they operate, teaching vocabulary as required.

3   Put the students in pairs. Give one copy of Cartoon A and one copy of Cartoon B to each pair. Each student has one cartoon and they cannot show their partner their cartoon.

4   Students describe their machine in detail to their partner, who attempts to draw it. At the end they compare drawings with the originals.

Processes, procedures, and operating systems | **93**

5 Ask students to think of domestic jobs and tasks they don't like doing—for example, washing up, ironing, hanging out washing, walking the dog, looking after young children in their family, etc.

6 In pairs or small groups invent and design a machine in the style of the cartoons used in steps 1 and 2 that will do the job for them.

7 Display the finished designs on a board or wall.

Session 2

1 Announce that the class have been asked to build a flying machine for a national competition. The machine can be anything they want, from a simple kite to a manned rocket to Mars. The important thing is that they, the students, have to make all decisions and that everyone must be involved. A detailed action plan of how to proceed (including a programme of work—see 4.9, 'Keeping to schedule') needs to be drawn up and submitted to the competition authorities within 40 minutes. You, as teacher, will not be involved, except to ensure that English is used as the language of communication during the task.

2 Tell students you are going to leave and you will return in five minutes to check they have decided on the type of machine they are going to build and have begun to organize roles and tasks. Withdraw from the room.

3 Return after five minutes and check they are working on something. It doesn't matter how they have organized things—one person may have taken control, or people may have decided to work on their own or small groups (although one hopes that they will have decided to work as a team). Check that clear procedures and plans of action are being established.

4 After 30 minutes, give the group a ten-minute warning, *The detailed action plan to be submitted by the class must be ready in ten minutes.*

5 Collect the action plans. The activity can stop at that point. Alternatively, depending on how realistic and achievable the project is, you can continue to the construction phase.

Variation

Rather than designing a flying machine, the activity could be to make a documentary (or promotional video) about their place of work. You should still leave it up to them to decide everything.

Follow-up

See if it flies!

5
Using numbers and figures

Numbers and figures are important in ESP teaching, not just in those specialisms with a clear numerical or technological basis (construction, commerce, science, and so forth) but also in service-based and people-based specialisms. Whatever the product or service they are working with, students will need to use numbers and present number-based data at some point in their work, and everyone will want to be paid and therefore understand the figures on their payslip or tax form!

One of the main challenges will be to get students speaking and thinking about numbers in English. Numbers are deeply ingrained in the mother tongue. Even very advanced students will often count in their first language, and for all levels the gap between the technical knowledge of the subject specialism and knowledge of English may be greatest when it comes to manipulating numbers and understanding numerical concepts. On top of this is the fact that numbers, while very similar in their written form across language borders, can have subtle but important differences—for example, continental Europe 25.000 vs UK 25,000; the different way in which number strings such as telephone numbers are broken up (20 8340 0828 vs 20 83 40 08 28). Many of the activities described here therefore emphasize features such as pair and group work, working things out aloud, and dictating calculations.

The first group of activities (5.1, 'Number warmers' to 5.6, 'Silly dimensions') provide practice of numbers in a variety of forms, including phone numbers, dates, specifications, and dimensions. In some of these activities, and in 5.7, 'Insurance claim dictation' and 5.8, 'Renovation project', teamwork with a competitive edge is encouraged as a way of maximizing oral practice of numbers and figures. The final activity (5.9, 'Are you paid what you're worth?'), takes a fairly light-hearted approach to the all-important area of pay, salary, tax, and financial value and reward.

5.1 Number warmers

Level   Elementary to advanced

Time   10–15 minutes—longer for Activity 3

Aims   LANGUAGE   Ordinal and cardinal numbers; symbols; dates; phone numbers; and other everyday numbers and figures.

OTHER   To break the ice and introduce the idea of numbers.

Sample topic   General

Transfer   The activities can work as warmers with any group, but you can choose items that will be especially relevant to the specialism you are teaching.

Preparation

Prepare cards of symbols/words for Activity 3.

Procedure

Activity 1

Students get in order of birthday (January to December), by mingling and asking everyone when their birthday is. This practises ordinals, '*th*' sound, and months.

Activity 2

Students collect each other's phone numbers, by mingling and noting down numbers (or entering them into their mobile if they have it). Practises pronunciation of digits, and listening for accuracy. (Input different conventions for number strings if you want—particularly valuable if you have a multinational class, or in contrast to UK/US norms.)

Note   Students may not be comfortable giving out their real numbers, so tell them they can invent if they want.

Activity 3

1   Give out a set of cards, half with symbols and abbreviations associated with numbers on them—%, $, £, mm (millimetre), km2 (square kilometres), @ (at a cost of—difficult!), x (multiplied by), * (multiplied by on an Excel spreadsheet formula), ÷ (divided by), °C (degrees centigrade), . (decimal point), _ (underscore—for email addresses),/(slash), and the other half with the written word—percentage, etc.

2   Shuffle the cards and spread them out face down on the table. Students have to turn over matching pairs of symbol and word. If they get it wrong, they have to turn them face down again.

Variation

Activity 1

Use other criteria—for example, distance travelled to get to class, furthest place you've ever been to, length of service in current job.

Activity 2

Students collect postal addresses or email addresses (not so many numbers, but still using number in context). Input on different international conventions, if you want—for example, position of house number in address, pronunciation of email symbols and web addresses.

Activity 3

When all the cards have been turned over, students make a question for each (for example, *What percentage of your income do you spend on rent?*). Go round and ask the others your questions.

5.2 Important numbers

Level	Elementary to advanced	
Time	30–40 minutes	
Aims	LANGUAGE	All types of numbers; prepositions with numbers and dates, question forms.
	OTHER	To break the ice and give general personalized practice of numbers and figures; to contextualize numbers and figures used in the specialism in a dialogue.
Sample topic	General	
Transfer	Activity can be used with all specialisms—adjust dialogue openings in step 5 to suit your specialism.	
Materials	Copies of opening lines of dialogues for step 5.	

Preparation

Copy and cut up opening lines of dialogues for step 5.

Procedure

1 On the board write five or six numbers, figures, or dates that are important to you (for example, phone number, birthday, house number, lucky lottery numbers, the number of the bus you take to work, the time of the train you take to work, how many hours you work a week, etc.). Obviously, you don't have to use the real numbers if you are concerned about privacy.

2 Ask students to guess what the numbers might represent.

3 In pairs, get the students to do the same for their own personal numbers and explain their significance to their partner.

4 In pairs, get students to write down five or six numbers, figures, or dates that could appear in their specialism. They could be the specification of a machine or computer, the date of an important meeting, or a hotel room number.

5 Distribute opening lines of a number of dialogues for the students to match.

> Have you got the model number of that printer?
> Yes, it's an HP 5150.
> Are you going to call the engineer to repair it?
>
> Which room is Professor Williams staying in?
> Room 803.
> Is that on the eighth floor?

Students then continue the dialogues—either written or spoken—using as many numbers and dates as possible (there must be at least one number in each utterance).

Variation

Do the dialogue step as a 'consequences' game (written or spoken), with students passing the dialogues around in a circle, adding one line at a time, but only seeing or hearing the previous line.

Follow-up

Produce a 'Numbers reference chart', listing the different conventions for writing and pronouncing numbers—for example, phone numbers vs money numbers vs hotel rooms vs specification numbers (or whatever forms are common in the specialism). You can start by looking at the different way 'o' is spoken—'oh' in phone numbers and hotel rooms, 'zero' in scientific contexts, 'nil' in sports scores (but 'love' in tennis), etc.

5.3 Predicting numbers

Level	Elementary to advanced
Time	30 minutes
Aims	LANGUAGE Numbers—*How much? How many*; question words (Variation 2).
	OTHER To develop awareness of different number types in context of a reading activity.
Sample topic	General
Transfer	Adapt the text to the specialism. For example, tour guides—commentary with dates, number of rooms in a palace, population figures, prices, etc. Motor mechanics—specification and performance comparison of two cars.
Materials	Photocopies of chosen text with gaps—one per student.

Preparation

Find an authentic text from the specialism (or write your own), which includes a range of numbers which should be relatively easy to insert according to knowledge of the specialism and common sense (see example on computer games).

Procedure

1 Write the numbers you have removed from the text on the board. Check students understand the different forms: percentages, fractions, ordinals, etc.

2 Give title of text and ask students to discuss what the numbers might refer to.

3 Give out the gapped text and get students to put the numbers in the correct place.

4 Check answers.

Example Numbers to be gapped are in bold—note: some of the numbers could be interchangeable, for example, *under 15/under 16*, but the ones given are the correct ones from the article.

Playing the game

According to the Department of Trade and Industry, children play games for an average of **45 minutes** a day.

The global games market is estimated to be worth more than **$17bn**. In Britain, almost **40m** games were sold last year for over **£934m**.

The Video Standards Council says that less than **1%** of games are classified as suitable for people aged **over 18**, while **90%** are suitable for children **under 15**.

The best selling computer game ever is Myst, in which players solve puzzles as they explore an imaginary world. It sold **5.5m** copies worldwide.

More than **two-thirds** of children prefer playing games with friends to playing alone.

The average age of gamers is **28**, but over **40%** of all console players are **under 16**.

('Zap! Go to the top of the class', *Guardian*, 24 March 2001)

Photocopiable © Oxford University Press

Variation 1

Depending on the text you choose, spend time at the start generating interest in the subject and hypothesizing about quantities involved. For example, for the sample text you might want to discuss the students' own experiences of playing computer games, including the age at which they started playing, how long they play/played for, how much time they spend/spent playing with friends, etc.

Variation 2

Set the activity up as an information gap, with students A and B having different numbers and gaps. This is good for practising quantity questions (*How much ...? How many ...? What proportion ...?* etc.), and you should do some presentation work on this if necessary.

Follow-up

Get students to make their own gap-fills of similar texts, and test them on other students.

5.4 Graphs and statistics

Level   Pre-intermediate to advanced

Time   40–50 minutes

Aims   LANGUAGE   Language of statistics and graphs, for example, trends, verbs of increase and decrease (*rise, drop, fall, grow,* etc.), adverbs (*gradually, steadily, dramatically,* etc.).

   OTHER   To practise the language of graphs, charts and statistics; to discuss the best way of presenting different types of information and data.

Sample topic   Tourism

Transfer   Focus on the graphs, charts, and data presentation forms that are most used in the specialism you are teaching.

Materials   Photocopies of 'Chart list'—one per pair/group.

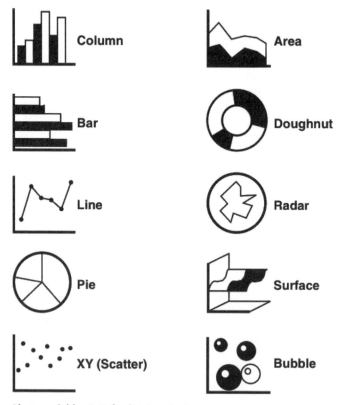

Column

Area

Bar

Doughnut

Line

Radar

Pie

Surface

XY (Scatter)

Bubble

Photocopiable © Oxford University Press

Preparation

1 Research some specialism-related data (graphs and charts).

2 Copy the 'Chart list'.

Procedure

1 As a class, brainstorm the different types of data that are used in the specialism.

Example In Tourism and travel this might be:
- International passenger arrivals
- Reasons for travelling
- Tourism as a percentage of GDP in different countries
- Average monthly temperatures/rainfall/hours of sunshine in a resort
- Occupancy rates in a hotel
- Levels of client satisfaction.

2 Divide the class into pairs or small groups and give out a copy of the 'Chart Wizard'. Ask the students to decide which of the graphs or charts would be suitable for each of the data items you brainstormed. If there are any of the charts not used by the data items you brainstormed, get them to try to think of data that might fit them.

3 Introduce one or two examples of graphs and charts from the specialism—for example, the increase in international passenger arrivals since 1950 (available from World Tourist Organization website). Use the examples to teach the language of graphs.

4 In pairs/groups, get students to choose two or three of the charts and data types and produce some actual statistics relevant to their subject. They can either research them (for homework or from the 'Authentic materials bank' in 1.6) or invent them. Inventing—though perhaps difficult, particularly for pre-work students—is not necessarily the weaker option, as the students should discuss the data (and thus use the language of numbers) to ensure they are as accurate and as reasonable as possible.

5 Students then pair up with individuals from other groups and dictate their data and graphs to each other. The partner has to listen carefully and draw the graph or chart without looking at the original. At the end they can compare the drawn graph with the original, and also compare with the authentic graphs and charts that you have researched.

Variation 1

You may want to restrict the number of graph and chart types to a few that are particularly relevant to your subject.

Variation 2

You can start with sets of raw data (i.e. not in graph or chart form) and get students to dictate this to other students, who must then decide how best to present the data.

Follow-up

A range of graphs and charts like this can be a visually attractive
feature, so display them on the class noticeboard, or in a class folder,
adding to them whenever further data comes up.

5.5 Specification bingo

Level	Elementary to advanced
Time	30 minutes
Aims	LANGUAGE Numbers in specifications; comparatives and superlatives.
	OTHER To practise figures and numbers from the specialism, with particular emphasis on listening skills.
Sample topic	Engineering—aircraft
Transfer	Activity can be transferred to any technical specialism by using a series of relevant parallel specifications. For non-technical specialisms use other figures, for example, costs, dates, prices, etc.
Materials	Photocopies of parallel texts with different specifications, to be used as bingo cards—one per student.

Preparation

Write down a range of numbers and figures including the ones on the
specification charts below, but with extra distractors.

Planes in the British Airways fleet

Plane	Boeing 747-400
Capacity	359 passengers
Range	11,485 km
Engines	RB211-524
Cruising speed	927 kph
Length	70.7 m
Wingspan	64.8 m

Plane	Airbus A321
Capacity	194 passengers
Range	3,692 km
Engines	IAE V2533-A5
Cruising speed	853 kph
Length	44.5 m
Wingspan	34.1 m

Plane	Boeing 737-500
Capacity	110 passengers
Range	2,172 km
Engines	CFM56-3C1
Cruising speed	815 kph
Length	31 m
Wingspan	28.9 m

Plane	Boeing 767-300
Capacity	181 passengers
Range	9,409 km
Engines	RB211-524
Cruising speed	873 kph
Length	54.9 m
Wingspan	47.6 m

Photocopiable © Oxford University Press

Procedure

1 Write some of the numbers from your prepared list on the board. Practise pronunciation with the class.

2 Give out the bingo cards and check students understand each of the categories, and know what any symbols or abbreviations represent.

3 For the first few numbers, appoint yourself as the caller and read out numbers and figures from your prepared list. Students cross them off their bingo card.

4 Call up students to take turns at being the caller, reading from your prepared list. This will allow them to practise their productive skills. (They will need to check their own card at the same time.)

5 The winner is the first student to complete their card.

6 Get the students in groups to look at their completed cards and make comparisons between the different specifications.

Example The Airbus A321 has a greater capacity than the Boeing 767-300 as it can take 13 more passengers.

Variation

The cards can also be used for a number of other activities:
• conventional gap-fill information gaps
• running dictations
• phone dictations (see 5.7, 'Insurance claim dictation')
• conventional dictations.

Follow-up

Get students to consider the application of the different items: *What or who are each of the specs best suited for (for example, for flights, long-haul or short-haul)? How would you present them and promote them to customers and clients?* (Exact application will depend on the specialism.)

5.6 Silly dimensions

Level Pre-intermediate to advanced

Time 50 minutes

Aims LANGUAGE Dimensions (length, area, volume); calculations: *multiplied by, divided by, A times B equals C, etc.*; comparatives and superlatives.

OTHER To practise language of dimensions and calculations.

Sample topic General

Transfer Activity can be used with any specialism. Some examples are given in step 9.

Materials Calculators—one per pair, a range of small and large items (visuals or real objects, as appropriate)—some examples are suggested in the chart.

Preparation

Collect a range of small and large items—some examples are suggested in the chart below. You could use visuals or real objects, as appropriate.

	Small	Big
Length	pencil tennis racket person match-stick	longest wall in classroom Eiffel tower (or other tall building) distance from home to work distance from where you live to London (or New York, or anywhere) circumference of the world (40,000 km)
Area	surface of desk floor of classroom CD case coursebook	football pitch area of own country area of USA area of world (148 million sq km)
Volume	matchbox bar of chocolate brick football (it's round but occupies more space so be careful!)	your car classroom a swimming pool St Paul's Cathedral (or other famous building) the world

(A brick or a double-decker bus can be used for length, area, and volume)

Procedure

1 Write on the board (or just say) a 'silly' fact.

Example *If you laid the entire human population of the world end to end they would go round the earth thirty times.*

2 With the class, brainstorm short items and write them in a column.

Example pencil, desk, person

3 Draw another column and brainstorm items that are very long and write them in the second column.

Example the longest side of the classroom, the distance from where you're studying to London, the length of your country, the circumference of the world

4 Take a simple example from each column and calculate how many of the small items would fit into the length of the long item. For example, *How many pencils would fit into the length of the longest side of the classroom?*

5 Focus on language items that you use:

Example One metre *divided by* 15 centimetres *equals* 6.7; *therefore* 6.7 pencils will fit in one metre.

The *length* of the wall is five metres; so 6.7 *multiplied by* 5 *gives a total of* 33.5 pencils.

6 In pairs, get students to calculate other pairs of items from the two columns. Make sure that one student makes the calculations verbally and the other writes them down (to ensure spoken practice of the target language takes place in English rather than the first language). A calculator can be used for the bigger and more difficult numbers, but make sure the students say the numbers to each other rather than just show the calculator display.

7 Compare results in class.

8 Repeat the same steps with area and then with volume.

9 Now get the students to relate this idea to their own specialism, if appropriate.

Examples
- Bricklayers—bricks in a wall, paving stones on a pavement.
- Teachers—students in a classroom.
- Travel agents (or anyone using printed display material)—brochures on a rack, or stored in a store cupboard.
- Motor mechanics—cars in a garage.
- Nurses/Doctors—beds in a ward/hospital, medicines in a cupboard.

Variation

A similar approach can be taken to timescales, for example, the history of earth compared to a single day.

Follow-up

This activity could lead into 5.8, 'Renovation project'.

5.7 Insurance claim dictation

Level Intermediate to advanced

Time 30–40 minutes

Aims LANGUAGE Telephone language; checking and clarifying.

OTHER To practise describing and understanding a range of number-based information, in an insurance claim/telephoning context.

Sample topic General, but with an emphasis on Business and commerce.

Transfer Insurance claims should be relevant in most specialisms.

Materials Photocopies of 'Insurance inventory form' (Worksheet 5.7) with first line completed—two per student.

Preparation

Photocopy two copies of Worksheet 5.7 per student.

Worksheet 5.7					
Quantity Item		Brief description	Model no. or specification	Other information (for example, size, colour)	Value
1	computer	Dell Dimension 3000	D001432672	Black, 1800mm x 3600mm x 3600mm	£495

Procedure

1 Get students to think about the place where they work—their desk, work station, bench, or room—and list all the items that are there (equipment, tools, computer).

2 Ask the students to imagine that there has been a fire and all the items have been destroyed. The insurance company needs a full inventory of the items to be claimed for and their replacement value.

3 From the list they drew up in step 1, students complete the insurance inventory form.

4 In pairs, the students dictate their insurance forms over the phone (i.e. sitting back to back) to their partner, who should then read it back to check the information is correct.

5 Students compare the two versions for accuracy.

Variation

'Phone dictations' like these can be used for other information types: for example, describing a graph or diagram, giving sales figures, a excel spreadsheet formula bar, etc.

Follow-up

1 Write the accompanying letter or email that would be sent with the claim form—for example, giving explanation of what happened.

2 Write the response from the insurance company (for example, asking for more information, accepting or rejecting the claim).

5.8 Renovation project

Level Pre-intermediate to advanced

Time 30–40 minutes (Set-up), ongoing project with 20 minute final report back session

Aims LANGUAGE Language of measurement and calculation; making suggestions and proposals.

OTHER To practise numbers, dimensions, measurements and calculations in the context of a broader project.

Sample topic Construction and building trades

Transfer Activity can be transferred to any specialism where teamwork is important.

Materials Photocopies of Report form—one per student; tape measures, rulers, and calculators (optional).

Procedure

1 As a warmer, and in order to check the students can use the language of measurement and calculation, divide the class into pairs. One member of each pair should measure the dimensions of the room you are in as quickly as possible and using whatever equipment they have (ruler, paces, visual), and then report back to their partner, dictating the dimensions. It is important that the measurer doesn't simply write down the measurements and give them to their partner, so monitor this carefully. Students compare answers.

2 Divide the class into four groups (or fewer if you have less than eight students). Give each group one of the following tasks for the building where they are studying:
- to replace all the windows
- to replace all the flooring
- to replace all the computers and IT equipment
- to replace all the furniture.

3 Each group should fill in the Report form.

Report form

What we'll need: _____

_____

Materials, equipment, and quantities:_____

_____

Manpower and time: _____

_____

Estimated costs: _____

_____

Photocopiable © Oxford University Press

They will need to go round and make the actual measurements (and gather the actual equipment to do the measuring, unless you are providing this yourself). This could take place over several days, as an ongoing project.

Do not give the students any additional instruction or guidance—it is up to them how they organize the task. The only thing is that they should be as accurate as possible. Of course, you can be available to answer any questions they have, and also to check language.

4 When the groups have finished the task and prepared the reports, ask them to regroup with one member from each of the original groups and show their reports. The new groups should put together a full proposal for renovation of the building.

Variation 1

You could substitute the students' places of work for the building where they are studying.

Variation 2

If you think the building tasks suggested above are not going to be very interesting or relevant to your students, you can set different tasks. Here are some suggestions:
- Organizing a party to celebrate the 25th anniversary of your company (budget, timing, schedule, etc.).
- Arranging for a work experience teenager to come for a week (their schedule, the costs involved, etc.).
- Robbing a bank (calculations of exactly where things are, for example, what walls have to be broken through, timing, how much money you'll get, and how you'll divide it).

Follow-up

Write up the renovation plans as a formal proposal, either as a letter plus report or an email plus report as attachment.

5.9 Are you paid what you're worth?

Level Pre-intermediate to advanced

Time 40–50 minutes

Aims LANGUAGE Vocabulary of salaries, wages, tax, benefits and deductions.

OTHER To practise figures, numbers, and calculations in the context of rates of pay, tax, and deductions.

Sample topic General

Transfer Activity will be of particular relevance to Business and commerce, but everyone needs to be able to understand invoices and payslips.

Materials Some examples of (blank) invoices or payslips, particularly for pre-work students.

Procedure

1 Introduce a discussion, either in open class or in pairs/groups, on these questions:
   - Are you paid enough?
   - Do you work too many hours?
   - Is there any work that you do that you are not paid for?
   - Should you be paid for it?
   - Do you pay too much/not enough income tax?
   - What other deductions do you pay—for example, national insurance, health benefits, pension contributions?

   Pre-work students could talk about a part-time or holiday job.

2 On their own, get students to think back over the past month (or week if you want to keep it simpler), and make a list of all the work they've done—not just in their job, but also housework, homework and study, helping others, etc.—and how many hours they've spent on each.

3 In pairs, get students to decide what they think a fair rate of pay is for each of the items, and what a fair rate of tax should be (or if the item should be tax exempt). They should also add expenses they have incurred in relation to the itemized work, and any deductions (health insurance, pension, etc.) that they feel should be made.

4 Get students to prepare an invoice or payslip for their services for the last month, including all items, tax, deductions, expenses, etc.

5 To finish the activity, find out who has 'earned' the highest net income.

Variation 1

Obviously some of this information will be sensitive and personal, but try to encourage a light-hearted approach to the activity and allow students to be 'economical with the truth'. Alternatively, you can get the students to do the whole activity for someone they know (friend or family), or a famous person (for example, a top footballer or the Prime Minister).

Variation 2

You may want to leave out the costing of housework and homework, as it raises wider issues. However, it is intended to make the activity more light-hearted and soften some of the sensitivity and intrusion that might otherwise be restrictive.

Follow-up

Write a letter asking your boss for a pay rise (or reduction!) on the basis of the calculations you have made.

6

Customer care and quality assurance

Looking after customers and clients and monitoring quality of service touch every business, and every specialism, in some form. In many fields of work it is the factor that gives the competitive edge. Even in specialisms where the customer is not very apparent or even non-existent, the activities in this chapter will have general use and significance: at root they relate to how we deal with, and work with people in everyday interactions, including colleagues and members of the public.

The focus in this chapter is on customer care through face-to-face interaction, although telephoning and writing skills are included. Many of the activities include an element of performance as well as interaction, and drama techniques will be very useful when covering this topic. Also, to fit in with the ethos of customer care, and especially quality control and quality assurance, there is a strong element of judging and assessing.

Knowing who the customers are, what their needs and desires are, and how to care for them effectively is the basis of the first group of activities (6.1, 'Best practice: personal experiences and customer identity' to 6.5, 'Dream Fulfilment Incorporated'). The next group of activities (6.6, 'Softening language' to 6.8, 'Customer care or customer control?') focuses on handling difficult situations, such as complaints and anger. Feedback and customer questionnaires and surveys are the subject of the next activity (6.9, 'Questionnaires and surveys'), and the final activity (6.10, 'Flight attendant role-play') brings together all the elements of the other activities and gives an extended focus on both customer care and quality assurance.

6.1 Best practice: personal experiences and customer identity

Level Pre-intermediate to advanced

Time 50–60 minutes (or two sessions of 30 minutes)

Aims LANGUAGE Imperatives *'do's'* and *'don'ts'*; contrasting registers: spoken vs written, formal vs informal.

OTHER To introduce the idea of customer care and 'best practice' in relation to the students' own personal experiences; to establish the identity of customers and clients within a specialism, and relate best practice ideas to specific situations.

Sample topic Marketing

Transfer Activity relates directly to any specialism where customers are involved, and indirectly to any situation where there is person-to-person interaction.

Procedure

Session 1

1 Give a personal example of when you received very good customer service—maybe in a restaurant or on a helpline (invent if necessary!).

2 Get students to think of their own good experiences as customers. Prompt with likely situations: in a restaurant, in a shop, on holiday, on the phone (or a help-line).

3 In pairs, students share their experiences and try to identify what it was that made the service good.

Example The person listened to me, the person anticipated my needs, the person was quick and efficient.

4 In pairs, students use the information to compile a list of 'Best practice for customer care'.

5 Pairs report back to the whole class.

6 Repeat the same steps, but for examples of bad experiences and worst practice.

7 Use the information and ideas to produce a *'Do's* and *don'ts* charter' for customer service. Keep this charter for the next session so that it can be used to refer to when looking at customer care in relation to the students' specialism.

Session 2

1 Write the question *Who are our customers?* on the board.

2 Choose a job that all students will know about, such as teacher, and identify the customers. Complete the chart below on the board by eliciting ideas from the students. Get the students to think not just of the obvious customers (students, children), but also indirect customers (parents, company sponsors).

Customer	Needs	Situation	Interaction
adult student	to learn the subject	lessons in class; homework/course assignments	face-to-face written marking (and spoken feedback)
children	general education, social skill, discipline, etc.	lessons in class; supervision outside class	face-to-face; some written
company sponsor	to know their employee is being taught well and is making progress	reports (written and spoken)	written reports; some phone calls
parent	to know their child is being taught well and is making progress	reports, parents' evenings	written reports, face-to-face, possibly phone calls

3 In small groups, students complete a similar chart for the customers/clients in their specialism, and then compare information with the class. Encourage them to have a wide interpretation of 'customers' and if necessary break them into sub-categories.

Example *Marketing and advertising*
- existing long-standing customers
- existing more recent customers
- potential new customers
- former customers
- people you need services from (for example, printers, venue managers, web consultants).

4 Relate the 'Do's and *don'ts* charter' from Session 1 to the grid, by adding a 'do's' and a '*don'ts*' column.

Example When talking to long-standing customers always start with some personal small-talk that shows you remember who they are.

Variation

For pre-work students, in Session 2 you may have to give out an already-completed grid for the specialism.

Follow-up

1 Collect examples of 'Customer care charters', both from within the specialism and from outside. Use them to compare with the charters that the students produce.

2 For more advanced students, focus on the language used in different registers—formal/informal, written/spoken. Develop into a role-play using situations/interactions from the grid that they have experienced. The exact situation and the people involved should be noted and then the students carry out role-plays in threes, with two

people acting out the situation and the third noting language used (for later analysis).

6.2 The customer journey

Level   Intermediate to advanced

Time   50–60 minutes

Aims   LANGUAGE   Dealing with enquiries; giving and confirming information; making and dealing with complaints; using appropriate register.

OTHER   To analyze and practise customer service at each step of the interaction between customer and provider; to introduce quality control and quality assurance techniques.

Sample topic   Tourism—hotels and hospitality

Transfer   Activity can be transferred to any specialism. Ensure the mode of interaction for each step is in keeping with what really happens in the specialism.

Preparation

Research the detailed stages of 'the customer journey' for the specialism you are teaching.

Procedure

1   For the specialism you are teaching, identify each stage of the interface between the customer and the provider (of the service or product). You can either elicit this from the students (preferred option if students have knowledge of their specialism), or prepare it yourself beforehand. An example for a hotel guest is given on the next page and this can be used if your students come from a range of specialisms, or if they do not know their product or service very well.

2   Discuss with the class what the customer wants, in general, at each of the stages you have identified. Also discuss not only what they expect, but ways in which they can be pleasantly surprised.

3   Divide the class into groups of three. Give each group one of the stages (or more than one, depending on the numbers of students and stages—but the stages you give should be in sequence).

4   Get the groups to discuss in detail what the customer wants and what is best practice at their stage. They should agree goals and quality targets—for example, to show interest in the customer, to find out exactly what the customer wants, to be quick and efficient, etc.).

5   Position the groups around the room in the order of the stages. Get them to write a sign showing the stage they are representing. Each member of the group takes on a different role: A is the provider, B is the customer, and C is the quality controller or monitor.

The customer journey through a hotel booking

- Making an initial search for hotels in the area (for example, on Internet)
- Making an initial enquiry and contact with the chosen hotel (for example, by phone or email)
- Making a definite reservation and receiving confirmation
- Arriving at the hotel and checking in
- Receiving information on the room and the facilities in the hotel
- Using various basic facilities (for example, bathroom, bed, restaurant, etc.)
- Using extra facilities (for example, sports facilities, spa, car hire)
- Asking for information during the stay
- Making a complaint
- Checking out
- Making post-service contact (for example, feedback questionnaire, further offer)

6   They should act out the interface they have discussed, with C making notes on whether agreed targets and goals are achieved. For stages that have direct provider-customer contact, the mode of interaction should simulate what happens in reality (for example, face-to-face, by phone, in writing). For stages such as 'searching for initial information', the contact can be more of a discussion (*We have a website and a brochure … We optimize our position on search engines by …*, etc.).

7   The Bs (the customers) then move onto the next stage and act out the new interface. As and Cs stay where they are.

8   When all stages are complete, students return to their original groups and discuss the different levels of care and quality assurance they encountered.

9   Whole class feedback on what the students have learnt from the activity.

Variation

The activity can be simplified by keeping the students in their original group of three and taking turns to play the three different roles for each stage. However, the sense of 'journey' will be lost, and there will be less contact with different 'customers'.

6.3 Smiling on the phone

Level All levels

Time 15–20 minutes

Aims LANGUAGE Intonation patterns.

OTHER To establish the fundamental customer service technique of smiling when you're talking to someone, even when on the phone.

Sample topic General

Transfer Activity can be used with any specialism where there is verbal customer interface, but also provides useful practice for anyone who has to use the telephone in their work.

Procedure

1 Write down some standard statements and two-line dialogues that could occur when making an enquiry or in a customer-provider situation.

Example
- Can I help you?
- Would you like me to send some information?
- Why don't you visit our website?
- Hold the line please.
- Can I take your name and number?

Students can add some expressions from their specialism.

2 Get the students to stand back to back with a partner.

3 Students take turns saying one of the sentences. For most of the sentences they should smile, but occasionally they should not. The partner has to spot when the speaker is smiling and when they are not—i.e. to 'hear the smile' in their voice.

Variation

This simple technique can be used to practise other intonation-based moods and registers—for example, polite/impolite, relaxed/stressed, caring/uncaring.

Follow-up

Use this activity as a warmer for any customer-provider dialogue practice.

6.4 Statement discussion

Level   Intermediate to advanced

Time   50–60 minutes

Aims   LANGUAGE   Giving opinions; turn-taking and turn-giving; agreeing and disagreeing.

OTHER   To discuss issues involved in customer care and quality assurance.

Sample topic   General

Transfer   Activity can be used with any specialism, but is best suited to people working in those which are service-based.

Materials   Photocopies of statement cards (see examples which can be adapted to fit your own situation)—one per group.

Preparation

Copy and cut up the statement cards.

Statement cards

The customer is always right.	It's important not just to *meet* customer expectations but to *exceed* them.	We don't have *customers*. We have *clients* and *colleagues*; 'customer' sounds too commercial.
Customer care is about delighting the client not just serving them.	If you are a customer, too much 'care' can be annoying: you just want the product and service, not lots of extras.	On average, satisfied customers tell two other people. Dissatisfied customers, on the other hand, tell nine other people.
Customers don't really know what they want, so it's OK to manipulate them and put pressure on them to buy something.	If customer service is really good, the customer will not notice it.	Managers must monitor their staff very closely when they are dealing with customers and be prepared to fire them if they are not doing it well.

Procedure

1 Write up the following definition of 'customer': '*An individual with a unique set of characteristics who buys or uses products or services*'. Ask the students if they think this is a good definition of the customers they meet in their specialism. Do customers always have a unique set of characteristics, or are there definite groups and types of customers whose needs you can predict? The purpose of this step is to get students into a discursive and opinion-giving frame of mind, and to bring out the language of discussion.

2 As the discussion continues, list the functions that will be useful for the later freer stages on the board.
- Giving opinions: *I think ..., In my opinion ..., If you ask me ...*
- Turn-giving: *What do you think, Jean? ... Peter, would you like to say something? ...*
- Turn-taking: *Can I just say something? ... Could I come in there? ...*
- Agreeing: *I agree ... Yes, that's a good point ... Exactly ...*
- Disagreeing: *I'm not so sure ... Sorry, I don't agree ...*

Model and practise the expressions you have listed.

3 Divide the class into groups of three or four. Give out a set of statement cards to each group. Ask the students to turn over one card at a time and discuss it for five minutes, giving their opinions and thinking of examples or case studies from their own experience where possible. One person per group should be responsible for keeping notes of the discussion.

4 After a suitable length of time (45 minutes), bring the class back together and report back briefly on one or two of the statements. Do any necessary language correction work.

Variation 1

For elementary students, simplify the language in the statements and shorten the list.

Variation 2

For students who need encouragement to discuss and give opinions, give out the lists of statements with four columns next to them, headed 'Agree', 'Disagree', 'Why', 'Examples/Case studies'. Pairs or groups complete the columns before moving to the open discussion at step 4.

Follow-up

Students prepare an extended presentation (or write an essay) on one of the statements.

6.5 Dream Fulfilment Incorporated

Level Intermediate to advanced

Time 30–40 minutes

Aims LANGUAGE Making suggestions; making plans.

     OTHER To discuss ways of meeting customer needs and wishes, and preparing practical steps to achieving them.

Sample topic General

Transfer By definition, a fantasy activity like this transcends the details of particular specialisms.

Materials Pieces of paper—2 or 3 per student.

Procedure

1 Give the students a personal example of something you've always dreamed of doing. It can be a complete fantasy or something more achievable.

Example Taking a trip to the moon, driving across the United States in a Mustang Convertible, playing football in front of a crowd of 50,000.

2 Get the class to discuss how you can be helped to achieve this dream—or how close you can get to it (for example, with the trip to the moon dream, the nearest might be a visit to a space centre, experience of weightlessness, and a flight in a high altitude plane).

3 Individually, the students write down two or three of their own dreams on separate pieces of paper.

4 Collect up the dreams and redistribute them to groups of three or four students (8–10 dreams per group). Tell the groups that they are a company called 'Dream Fulfilment Incorporated'. Their job is to help people achieve their dreams—or get as near to them as possible.

5 The groups look at each of the dreams in turn and decide how best they can help the client who has requested it. They should produce practical steps for the customer to follow. Here is a possible 'Dream fulfilment plan' for one of the examples given in step 1:

Example

Dream Fulfilment Plan

Client's dream: Drive across the USA in a Mustang Convertible

Step	Practical advice	Target date
1 Research timescale and route	Buy road maps of USA	
2 Plan budget	What will the exact cost be? How long will it take to save up?	
3 Book time off work	Follow usual company procedures— request extra time if necessary	
4 Research car hire companies at chosen start place, and accommodation en route	Internet, then phone. Note: you need a company that can collect the car at destination. The Automobile Association of America provides a good guide to accommodation.	
5 Book flights	Research best flight through Internet or travel agent	
6 Decide on in-car entertainment	Buy CD of your favourite music	

6   Redistribute the dreams and the fulfilment plans to the original 'dreamers', and find out if they are satisfied with the proposal.

Variation

Make the dreams specific to the specialism, either from the start of the activity or as a separate step.

Follow-up

Write the 'Mission statement and customer charter' for Dream Fulfilment Incorporated.

6.6 Softening language

Level Intermediate to advanced

Time 40 minutes

Aims LANGUAGE Language of complaining and dealing with complaints.

OTHER To identify and practise language used to 'soften' difficult situations.

Sample topic General

Transfer Activity can be used with any specialism where there is disagreement or need to deliver difficult news, but it is designed mainly for those which are service-based with direct customer-provider interface.

Materials Photocopies of dialogue prompts—one per student.

Preparation

Photocopy the Dialogue prompts.

Dialogue prompts

A We had a huge argument.

B What seems to be the problem?

C This jacket is totally ruined you clumsy idiot.

D Can't you see I'm talking to someone?

E Do you think you might have made a mistake?

F Sorry to keep you waiting madam. I'll be with you in a minute.

G You've got it completely wrong.

H I'm extremely sorry. I'll find out who's responsible immediately.

I What are you complaining about?

J Would you mind coming this way sir?

K I'm just going to be a little bit longer with this customer and then I'll be right over.

L Just wait, will you.

M There was a bit of a misunderstanding.

N I really don't think it's anything to do with us.

O I think there's a little stain, but I'm sure it'll wash off. Don't worry.

P Get over here!

Procedure

1 Give an example of a 'hard' and a 'soft' statement.

Example *This soup is cold.* vs *Excuse me, but I'm afraid this soup is a little cold.*

Ask the class what makes the second statement softer—for example, use of *excuse me*, *I'm afraid* and *a little*.

2 Give out the list of statements, and set the task. Students should:
a match up hard and soft pairs
b identify language features
c say whether the situation is one that could occur in their specialism.

3 Report back on the answers.

Pairings 'Hard' first (some room for other possibilities): A–M, I–B, C–O, D–K, G–E, L–F, N–H, P–J

Key language features
- Use of extreme adjectives and adverbs—*huge, totally, completely* vs *a little, a bit of, extremely*
- Euphemism—*an argument* vs *a misunderstanding*
- Softening verbs—*seems, might* (and other modals)
- Use of *I'll*—offers and action
- Abuse—*clumsy idiot* vs *sir, madam*
- Use of imperatives—sounds rude.

4 In pairs, get students to choose two or three of the statements and build a short dialogue related to their specialism.

5 Ask one or two of the pairs to act out their dialogue for the rest of the class, who can comment on whether the language should or could be softened any further.

Variation 1

For weaker students divide the statements into two columns, 'hard' and 'soft'. Students then only have to match across the columns.

Variation 2

The pairings step could be done as a mingling activity, with each student given one of the statements and then having to find their 'hard' or 'soft' partner.

Follow-up

The language focus of this activity can be used in 6.7, 'Dealing with complaints, anger and crisis'.

6.7 Dealing with complaints, anger and crisis

Level Intermediate to advanced

Time 40–50 minutes

Aims   LANGUAGE Question forms; *will* for offers; a variety of functional exponents (step 3).

        OTHER   To practise the language of handling complaints and crises.

Sample topic Tourism—hotels and hospitality

Transfer Activity can be transferred to any specialism. Choose written or spoken forms depending on which is most appropriate.

Preparation

Have some examples of things that can go wrong in the specialism—include a range, not just complaints, but crises and emergencies in general.

Procedure

1 Set the example context of a hotel. Identify things that can go wrong—not just customer interaction, but any work-related situation. Avoid health and safety issues, as they will feature in the activities in the next chapter. Concentrate on situations where there are complaints, anger, and crisis, such as an overbooked room or a room that hasn't been cleaned, an abusive guest or a power cut.

2 Establish the core behaviour that the service provider needs to exhibit: calmness, an ability to listen, sympathy, clear explanation, the offer of a solution or plan of action. Elicit the type of functional language that will be needed in these situations:

Example	
Initial reaction and apology	Oh dear. I'm sorry to hear that. I'm really very sorry. Is there a problem?
Asking for clarification	What exactly is the problem?
Taking details	I'll just take some details. Could you describe … Let me see if I can help. I just need a few details.
Offering an explanation	I'm terribly sorry, but there has been a bit of a problem. If I could just explain …
Proposing a plan	I'll see if I can sort it out. I'll tell you what I'll do. This is what I'll do … Why don't you …

3 Practise the forms that you think will be most appropriate for your specialism.

4 In groups, get students to think about similar things that can go wrong in their own field of work and write them on a piece of paper.

5 Get the students to exchange papers with another group. The groups then discuss the situations and complaints they have been given and decide how they will respond, what they will say, and what course of action they propose.

6 Ask students to form new groups of three and role-play two or three of the situations. The third person in each group should be the Quality Controller, whose job is to assess how the service provider handles the situation. Students should take turns to perform this role.

Variation

For more advanced levels instruct the complainers to act in different ways—for example, very vague, very aggressive, or simply not listening—in order to test the service provider's ability to get details, stay calm, or give explanations.

Follow-up

1 Write a report on one of the problem situations, describing what happened and how it was handled.

2 Make a telephone follow-up call (or send an email) to find out if the person who complained (or was affected by the situation) was happy with the way the complaint was handled.

6.8 Customer care or customer control?

Level   Pre-intermediate to advanced

Time   50–60 minutes

Aims   LANGUAGE Direct and indirect instructions (imperatives, *Could you …*, *I'm sorry but …*, *if* clauses for warning and advising); polite language; intonation work.

OTHER   To practise language of controlling or handling customers in situations which are potentially difficult or dangerous.

Sample topic   Tourism and travel—air travel

Transfer   Activity can be transferred to any specialism which involves dealing with customers or clients.

Materials   Photocopies of cartoons, dialogue (cut up) and Worksheet 6.8—one per student.

Preparation

Copy the cartoons and dialogues. Cut up the lines of dialogue.

Procedure

1 Use the cartoons to introduce the topic of dealing with angry or aggressive customers, or customers who need to be controlled in some way. Discuss general tactics for dealing with them.

2 Give out the dialogue on the next page (jumbled) and ask students to sequence it and identify the situation (passenger trying to board plane after departure gate has closed).

3 Focus on the language used in the dialogue by the airport official to control the passenger, and discuss which expressions are stronger or more polite. Point out how the dialogue shifts from indirect, polite statements and requests to more direct statements and instructions as the customer becomes more irate and uncooperative. Recap by writing the following exponents on the board, using the example of 'No smoking':

Language area	No smoking
Imperative	*Don't smoke here!*
Can you/Could you?	*Can you please not smoke here?*
I'm sorry/I'm afraid	*I'm sorry but you can't smoke here./I'm afraid this is a no smoking area.*
If clause	*If you want to smoke, you'll have to go to the special area.*

A Excuse me, sir. I'm sorry, but you can't go through there.

B Why not? We're going to miss the flight otherwise.

A I'm afraid you're too late—the cabin doors have been shut.

B But can't you open them? Surely they can let us in—we're only five minutes late.

A I'm afraid that's not possible. Once the cabin doors have been shut, no one can go on.

B That's ridiculous. What are we supposed to do? It's your stupid security procedures that made us late in the first place. We're going through anyway ... Come on ...

A Sir, do not go through the barrier! If you do, I'll have to call security.

B Hmmm. OK, if you insist.

A Thank you, sir. Now, if you see my colleague at the airline desk over there, she'll make sure that you get on the next available flight. You may not have to wait long—there's another flight in an hour or so.

B OK.

Photocopiable © Oxford University Press

4 Give out Worksheet 6.8—some similar situations in the form of a grid—and get students to complete it in pairs or groups (or complete the grid on the board as a whole class activity).

5 In pairs, get students to role-play the situations, taking turns to be the passenger or the airport/airline employee. Passengers should try to be as insistent as possible; employees as firm as necessary.

6 When the role-plays are finished, discuss with the class how they felt as an employee in the situations. Did they feel comfortable? Did they enjoy telling the passenger what to do?

Variation 1

The activity can be shortened by not having the dialogue jumbled, or by leaving out the analysis stage (step 4) and going straight to the role-play.

Worksheet 6.8

Situation	Why it's wrong	Possible reason for passenger's behaviour	Level of firmness required
Passenger not waiting behind line at immigration.			
Passenger not wanting to take off shoes at security check.			
Passenger refusing to open suitcase at customs.			
Passenger going through a door marked 'Private'.			
Passenger on a flight standing up when the seat-belt sign is on.			
Passenger on a flight ordering a drink when he/she is already a bit drunk.			
Think of another.			

Variation 2

For transfer to other specialisms, you could use the activity in a variety of ways:

- Use the cartoons at step 1 to introduce the idea of dealing with difficult customers, and then move directly into a dialogue appropriate to your specialism.

- Do steps 1–3, and then introduce situations from your own specialism at step 4.
- Do the whole activity as described below, and then after step 6 introduce similar situations from your own specialism and repeat the role-play at steps 5 and 6. This will obviously require more time—around 30–40 minutes for the additional role-play work.

Follow-up

Write a report on one of the problem situations, describing what happened and how it was handled.

6.9 Questionnaires and surveys

Level   Pre-intermediate to advanced

Time   50 minutes

Aims   LANGUAGE   Question forms; grading adjectives
(*excellent–good–fair/satisfactory–poor*).

OTHER   To analyze and design ways of discerning customer satisfaction.

Sample topic   General

Transfer   Activity can be used with any specialism. For those which do not have a clearly identifiable customer base, the questionnaire can be used more as an internal audit and quality survey, to see if an organization can improve efficiency and working practices.

Materials   Photocopies of examples of feedback questionnaires (ideally from the specialism)—one per student.

Preparation

Photocopy enough questionnaires for one per student.

Procedure

1   Get the class to think about the products and services that their specialism offers. *What type of feedback do you want to get from your customers and clients—the people who use the product and service?* Write the list on the board. *Why is such feedback important?*

2   Give out (or write up) the list of criteria opposite for feedback questionnaires, and get the students, in pairs or groups, to discuss the advantages and disadvantages of each and to put them in an order of priority.

3   Report back to whole class. Ask if there are any other ways of getting feedback (for example, phone sampling, focus groups), and discuss if they are better than questionnaires.

4   Divide the class into new groups and get them to look at the example questionnaires you have brought in and assess them, improving them by adding or deleting items according to points made in steps 1–3.

A feedback questionnaire needs to:

- be given out at the point of sale.
- be easy to fill in (for example, tick boxes rather than write sentences).
- be available online as well as in hard copy.
- cover all aspects of the service or product.
- have some sort of reward (so that people have an incentive to return it).
- be used for planning policy, not just filed away.

Photocopiable © Oxford University Press

5 In pairs, get the students to fill in one of the questionnaires.

6 You are going to use the completed questionnaire for a role-play, but first get the students to think about the criteria for carrying out a survey/questionnaire:

Write up the following seven criteria (adapt if you want), and discuss what you might say in each case:

Example
- Say what the questionnaire is about.
- Ask permission before you ask any questions.
- Tell the person how long the interview will last.
- It is not enough to ask polite questions. You have to sound polite too. This is easier if you smile when you ask the questions.
- Avoid looking down at your question sheet all the time. Remember to look at the person you are interviewing when you talk to them.
- Be interested in what the person is saying (but don't get sidetracked into a long conversation).
- Thank the person at the end.

7 Act out the role-play, either in pairs or as a mingling activity. Students can use the information they filled in on the written forms.

Variation 1

For elementary groups, the activity can be done with very simple questions and omitting steps 2 and 3. For higher levels and for extended project work, the students can design a whole range of feedback media—written, online, phone calls.

Variation 2

Get students to write their own questionnaires based on their own workplace and their knowledge of the specialism. Use these either instead of or as a comparison with the example questionnaires you have collected.

Variation 3

Bring out pairs of students to the front of the class to act out the survey in front of the other students. The other students are judges and should give scores out of five for each of the seven criteria you have established earlier. You could even do it like an ice-skating contest and get the students to hold up number cards for each of the criteria.

Follow-up

Write up the results of the questionnaires as a formal report.

6.10 Flight attendant role-play

Level	Intermediate to advanced
Time	60 minutes (including feedback discussion)
Aims	LANGUAGE Question forms; welcoming; giving instructions; dealing with complaints and problem situations.
	OTHER To practise professional language skills when under pressure and dealing with awkward customers.
Sample topic	Tourism—air travel
Transfer	Activity can be adapted to any specialism where service-providers are dealing with customers, clients, or the public in general.
Materials	Photocopies of role-cards; props such as trays and cups/glasses (optional).

Preparation

1 Copy two sets of role-cards, A and B. There should be three times more Bs than As.

2 Arrange furniture in class to look like the passenger section of an airplane, with an aisle and chairs close together. There should be enough chairs for all of group B, but no more.

3 Ensure a separate space (ideally a different room) for the two groups to prepare—it is important that they don't overhear each other.

Procedure

1 Introduce the class to the 'airplane'. Check they know what the different features are and point them out (although they are imaginary)—for example, aisle, window-seat, overhead locker, meal tray, and (most importantly) call button (although in the activity the 'passengers' will have to raise their hands to call the attendant).

2 Divide into two groups, A and B. There should be two or three times as many Bs as As. Separate the two groups (ideally in different rooms).

3 Give out the role-cards. Allow at least 15 minutes for the groups to prepare their roles. Both groups should make notes on their role-cards, and practise together what they are going to say. In particular,

Role A—Flight attendants

You have just completed your training and you are now a fully-qualified flight attendant. In the role-play you will show how good you are at your job. Make notes before you start.

Step 1	What to say and do
1 Greet passengers.	_____
2 Seat passengers.	_____
3 Stow baggage safely, check seat-belts, etc.	_____
4 Make safety announcements.	_____

Step 2	
1 Serve drinks before lunch.	_____
2 Serve lunch trays.	_____
3 Serve tea and coffee.	_____
4 Collect lunch trays.	_____
5 Offer goods for sale.	_____

Step 3	
1 Prepare for landing.	_____
2 Say goodbye.	_____

Role B—Passengers

You and the other passengers are really airline inspectors travelling in secret. It is your job to see how new flight attendants cope with the pressures of the job. As a team you have to work out the best way of testing each flight attendant. You can be frightened, worried, drunk, talkative, difficult to please, noisy, etc.

It is very important that the flight attendants do not realize who you really are. Act like a 'normal' passenger at first. It is probably best if you save most of your extreme behaviour until step 2. Make notes before you start.

Step 1	**What to say and do**
1 Greeting.	_____ _____
2 Seating.	_____ _____
3 Stowing baggage, fastening seat-belt, etc.	_____ _____ _____
4 Listening to safety announcement.	_____ _____

Step 2	
1 Drinks before lunch.	_____ _____
2 Lunch.	_____ _____
3 Tea and coffee.	_____ _____
4 Collection of lunch trays.	_____ _____
5 Offer of goods for sale.	_____ _____

Step 3	
1 Preparing for landing.	_____ _____
2 Saying goodbye.	_____ _____

group B (the 'passengers') should work as a team and not act angrily or aggressively too early on.

4 Bring the groups together to act out the role-play. The 'passengers' board the plane to be greeted and seated by the flight attendants. Your role is to collect errors (and examples of good practice) and maintain the momentum throughout (without interfering).

5 Make sure you follow each of the three steps in order. You may need to signal the next step. Allow approximately ten minutes for each.

6 End the role-play and reconvene the group. Together discuss these questions:
   - How well did the flight attendants cope with the pressure?
   - Work out some strategies for dealing with 'difficult' passengers.
   - Has the experience changed your ideas about the job of flight attendant in any way?

7 Go over any language errors you collected.

Variation 1

Give the passenger/inspectors specific items to complain about.

Variation 2

Use different situations for different specialisms. For example, restaurants (waiters and diners), hospitals (nurses and patients), guided tours (tour guides and tourists), and any transport situation. By turning group B into overt inspectors, this activity can also be used in production and construction vocations.

Follow-up

Write sections of a training manual or guidance notes on how to deal with different kinds of difficult customers.

Acknowledgements

This activity also appears in *Going International* (Keith Harding, OUP 1998).

7
Health and safety

Recognizing risks and dangers to health in the workplace and protecting employees from these risks are an important part of modern working practice. The responsibility for health and safety is shared by employers and employees alike, and will usually feature very early on in an employee's training and induction. It is important in all workplaces, but especially on building sites and in trades where machinery or dangerous substances are used. Offices, for example, are full of potential hazards—badly positioned furniture, electric cables, computer screens, and even cups of hot coffee.

The activities in this chapter aim to involve students actively in awareness of health and safety issues and their practical implementation. The language work involved is fairly closely defined by the topic, for example, modals, imperatives, advice, and conditionals, plus some reporting language (past tenses).

The vocabulary is fairly specific, with lexical sets on such areas as: dangers and hazards, injuries, and verbs such as slip/fall. As they are set in the context of daily routines and work practices, the activities will also give intensive practice of specialism vocabulary—so even if you do not consider health and safety to be a particular need for your students, it has a value by providing content language in a personalized context.

The activities will explore general health and safety awareness (7.1, 'Health and safety questionnaire' and 7.2, 'Don't panic'), and specific items and procedures such as warning labels and signs, first aid, accident books, and risk assessment (7.3, 'Read the label' to 7.7, 'Spot the danger—risk assessment'). There is also a hazard game (7.8, 'The dangerous workplace game') and an activity on disability awareness (7.9, 'Disability awareness').

One general idea that you can apply to the activities in this chapter—and indeed to any activity—is to appoint a Health and Safety Officer at the start of each lesson. Their role is to assess the potential danger in any activity that takes place (for example, tripping over electric cables, leaning back on chairs, maintaining a correct ambient temperature) and reminding the group of fire regulations and any other health and safety issues.

7.1 Health and safety questionnaire

Level Intermediate to advanced

Time 40–50 minutes

Aims LANGUAGE Question forms; general tense work.

OTHER To explore the concept of health and safety by putting it in the general context of lifestyle—health, safety, and security; to practise writing and answering surveys and questionnaires.

Sample topic General

Transfer Activity is particularly relevant to Marketing and advertising, Phone-based services, and Medicine.

Preparation

Prepare the two example questions for each survey, either to write on the board or on the top of a photocopiable worksheet.

Procedure

1 Write *Health* and *Safety* on the board. Underneath each write the questions: *How healthy are you? How safe are you?*

2 Lead some simple general discussion on the two questions. In particular, get the students to think about the different contexts for health (for example, at work, at home, in social life; exercise, nutrition, alcohol, sleep, working long hours) and safety (personal, corporate, national—for example, at home, on the street, at work, on the Internet).

3 Divide the class into two groups. One half will prepare a questionnaire on *How healthy are you?* the other half on *How safe are you?*

4 Give two starter questions for each group: see box opposite.

5 Get the students to write approximately six more questions for their topic, covering the different contexts identified in step 2.

6 When the questionnaires are complete, get the students to pair up with someone from the other group and conduct the questionnaires on each other.

7 Students then return to their original groups and discuss the results.

Variation 1

Focus the questionnaires specifically on health and security at their workplace (or place of study for pre-work students).

Variation 2

For elementary students, write the questionnaire yourself and focus on particular grammar areas—for example, present simple for routines and habits for the health questionnaire, and simple past and present simple for security.

Example

Health

1 How often do you take physical exercise?
 a Every day.
 b Once or twice a week.
 c Maybe once a month or so.

2 On average how many days sickness do you have in a year?
 a I'm never sick
 b Fewer than six.
 c Six or more.

Safety

1 Have you ever been burgled/robbed? How many times?
 a Never.
 b Once or twice.
 c Three times or more.

2 How often do you back up the data on your computer?
 a Never.
 b Whenever I remember.
 c Every day.

Follow-up

Write a report based on the findings of the surveys. Suggest ways in which people can live healthier and more secure lives.

7.2 Don't panic

Level Pre-intermediate to advanced

Time 30–40 minutes

Aims LANGUAGE Modals (*must, should, need*, etc.); imperatives; first conditional.

 OTHER To set the scene for dangerous situations and how to cope with them.

Sample topic General

Transfer Activity looks at universal dangers, but can include dangerous situations specific to the specialism.

Procedure

1 Ask the class if anyone has been stuck in a lift (or knows anyone who was). If there is anyone who hasn't been stuck in a lift, ask them what they would do if they were. Ask the people who have been stuck in a lift, if that is what they did.

2 Discuss what you should do/not do if you get stuck in a lift—and the consequences of these actions.

Example *If you get stuck in a lift, you should press the alarm and wait.*
If you press the alarm and wait, someone will rescue you eventually.
If you scream, it will make everyone else panic.

3 Get the students to brainstorm other potentially dangerous situations. For example, driving in thick fog, hearing a burglar downstairs, walking into the middle of a bank robbery, hearing a fire alarm.

4 In pairs, get students to write one of the situations on a piece of paper, and then pass it to the pair on their left, for example, *You hear a fire alarm.*

5 The pairs write down one thing to do, and one thing not to do in the situation on the piece of paper. They then pass it on to the pair on their left.

Example *You hear a fire alarm.*
You should leave the building immediately.
You shouldn't run.

6 The pairs make conditional sentences based on the things to do and not do.

Example *If you leave the building immediately, you will be safe.*
If you run, you may cause a panic or fall and injure yourself.

7 Continue passing the paper round, pairs add more things to do and not do, and conditional sentences, alternately, until they can't think of any more.

Variation 1

Instead of using the dangerous situations suggested, get students to think about the potential dangers of their everyday routine, both at home and at work, and imagine what could possibly go wrong.

Variation 2

For elementary students keep to modals and imperatives and avoid conditionals.

Follow-up

Students can prepare an advice sheet for public display: 'What to do and what not to do in the event of …'

7.3 Read the label

Level	Intermediate to advanced
Time	40–50 minutes
Aims	LANGUAGE Warnings—imperatives, passive infinitive.
	OTHER To understand safety instructions and health warnings; to write safety instructions and health warnings.
Sample topic	Horticulture and agriculture
Transfer	Activity can be transferred to Medicine (labels on drugs and medicines), Construction and building trades (tools), Mechanical trades and Engineering (machines and equipment).
Materials	Examples of safety and warning labels—cigarette packet, bleach etc.; examples of non-dangerous items—pencil, stapler, rubber, etc.; examples of dangerous items from the specialism—axe, chainsaw, herbicide, etc.

Procedure

1 Bring in a random collection of items with safety instructions and health warnings.

2 Get students to read out the labels, list the key language on the board in categories—it will probably be a mixture of imperatives (*Use as directed. Do not insert in ear.*), passive infinitives (*To be taken three times a day. Not to be given to children.*), and general warning statements (*Smoking kills!*).

3 Give out the non-dangerous items. Get students to think of appropriate, if unnecessary, warnings and safety instructions.

Example Stapler: *Use on paper only.*
Rubber: *Not to be eaten.*
Pencil: *Do not insert in ear or up nose.*

4 Divide the class into groups of three or four. Show or brainstorm, items that are potentially dangerous from their own specialism. If you are using real items, do not give them out because students will see the labels and instructions—they can compare their versions later. Get the students to write labels and safety instructions. You should check the contents and sub-headings on the real examples you have, to ensure that students are writing to the correct template, and pre-teach any important vocabulary. See example for horticulture and agriculture, where the sub-headings are: general description of use of product, contents, and precautions.

Example 1 (For elementary students)

Horticulture and agriculture
Axe
- Keep blade covered with protective hood when not in use.
- Always hold by the (covered) blade when carrying.
- When using make sure nobody is within a three metre range.
- Store in a secure cabinet or locker.

Example 2   (For higher-level students)   7.3

Herbicide

For the control of broad-leaved weeds in grassland and scrub control in forestry and uncropped areas.

Contents: an emulsifiable concentrate containing 200g/litre 2,4 D as the Ethyl Hexyl Ester, 85g/litre Dicamba and 65g/litre Triclopyr as the Buutoxyethyl Ester.

Precautions:
- Wear suitable protective clothing (coveralls), protective gloves, rubber boots and face protection (faceshield) when handling the concentrate.
- Wear suitable protective clothing (coveralls), protective gloves, rubber boots and face protection (faceshield) when applying by hand-held equipment and handling contaminated surfaces.
- Wear suitable protective clothing (coveralls) when applying by vehicle-mounted equipment.

For use only as an agricultural/horticultural and forestry herbicide.

Caution
Chemical irritants

Danger
Highly flammable

5   Compare the students' examples with the real ones.

Variation

Get students to label every item in the classroom with a safety instruction or warning sign—for example, window: *Danger! Fragile! Do not break with hand.*

Follow-up

Focus on vocabulary by looking through a range of examples from their specialism and listing useful words and phrases, for example, *harmful, irritating, flammable, handle, protective clothing, contaminated surfaces,* etc. Students can translate them into their own language or you can do some word-building activities (noun/adjective/verb).

7.4 Warning signs

Level Pre-intermediate to advanced

Time 30–40 minutes

Aims LANGUAGE Modals; shapes and colours; collocations.

OTHER To understand international warning symbols; to identify hazards specific to students' specialism.

Sample topic Construction and building trades

Transfer Activity can be transferred to any specialism where international warning and safety signs are used, but is particularly relevant to Construction and building trades, Engineering, Horticulture and agriculture, Mechanical trades, and Medicine and health care.

Materials Examples of warning signs—a photocopiable sheet for the construction and building trades is provided.

Preparation

Prepare four shapes: a green 'landscape' rectangle, a blue circle, another circle with red circumference and red diagonal line going from left down to right, and a yellow/orange triangle with black edge (point up).

Procedure

1 Show the four shapes. Check the language of shape (*circle, triangle, rectangle*) and colour.

2 Ask the class if the signs mean anything to them. They will probably identify the red circle (for example, for 'No smoking'). Encourage discussion on what the different colours might mean.

3 Get the students to match the shapes and colours to their meanings:
   a Prohibition (*stop, do not, must not, no*)—red circle
   b Mandatory (must obey)—blue circle
   c Warning (risk of danger or hazard)—yellow/orange triangle
   d Safe condition (information about safe conditions)—green rectangle.

4 Ask the students which shapes/colours would be used for these meanings (Construction and building trades):
   • Ear protection must be worn   (b)
   • Danger, electricity   (c)
   • No unauthorised persons   (a)
   • Fire exit   (d)

5 Focus on warnings. Give out a list of warnings that would be relevant to the students' specialism.

Worksheet 7.4 Construction and building trades

1 slippery floor

5 deep water

2 trip hazard

6 fork-lift trucks

3 falling objects

7 compressed gas

4 fragile roof

8 cleaning in progress

Caution
Cleaning in progress

If you like, you can do some work on collocations at this point—for example, get the students to match the adjectives with the nouns and think of other collocates (see 3.8, 'Corpora').

6 Give out the sheet of symbols and get the students in pairs to match them to the warnings. Check answers.

7 Put the students in groups and get them to think more generally about the dangers and warnings in their work situation, and to design suitable symbols—using all four categories. Encourage them not just to think about obvious hazards, but also unusual and amusing ones, for example, untidy desk, avoiding hot coffee, Monday morning, colleague in a bad mood, boss alert—in other words, all the areas where they have to be careful or take special action.

8 Get the students to compare their new symbols in class.

Variation

Use the classroom and the building where you are studying as the source of symbols—students can go round and look for them and report back, and then at the end of the activity suggest other areas in the building where symbols might be a good idea.

Follow-up

Use the work on warning symbols in 7.7, 'Spot the danger—risk assessment' and 7.8, 'The dangerous workplace game'.

7.5 First aid

Level Intermediate to advanced

Time 30–40 minutes

Aims LANGUAGE Vocabulary of parts of the body, injuries, and treatment; past tenses, third conditional; *should have/shouldn't have.*

OTHER To discuss emergency first aid.

Sample topic General

Transfer Activity can be used with any specialism, particularly those where there is an element of danger.

Procedure

1 Start with a personal anecdote of an injury you had and how you got it. Scars are also a good source of material.

2 Whatever anecdote you tell, it should generate a lot of language— lexical and grammatical. Categorize the vocabulary into three groups: parts of the body (tongue, ankle, knee, etc.); injury (swollen, sprained, broken); and treatment (injection, bandage, plaster). Work on the grammar if you want—narrative past tenses, third conditional, *should have/shouldn't have.*

3 In pairs, get the students to think of an accident or injury they have had and write down three things:
   • the injury/part of the body
   • the activity that caused the injury
   • where the injury happened.

4 Students exchange their piece of paper with their partner. They ask each other about the incident, particularly if anything could have been done to prevent it and if it was anyone's fault. They should also say what treatment they received for the injuries.

5 Report back on a few general injuries in class and discuss what you should do to treat them.

6 Get students to think specifically about the workplace. Ask them about injuries that can occur in their specialism and recommendations for healthy work practices. Get them to mix and match potential problems (aching wrists, back pain, eye strain, headaches, etc.) with good practices (change your position frequently, take a short break every hour, bend your knees when you lift things, etc.).

Variation

For pre-work students you can omit step 6. For in-service students you may want to focus on work-based injuries earlier on.

Follow-up

Prepare a 'First aid for the workplace' guide or poster, listing the possible injuries that can occur in their workplace or specialism, and what should be done to prevent them.

7.6 The accident book

Level   Intermediate to advanced

Time   50–60 minutes

Aims   LANGUAGE   Past tenses; third conditional; *should have/ shouldn't have*.

OTHER   To look at the language of accidents, their causes and how they are logged in the workplace; report writing.

Sample topic   Administration and office work

Transfer   Activity can be transferred to any specialism.

Materials   Photocopies of a story of a disaster or accident—one per student.

Preparation

Find or write a story about an accident that had disastrous consequences for a company or people working in the specialism. To write your own, you can still use the headline used in the example text, but adapt it to the workplace of the specialism—ensure that you include lots of examples of negligence and bad practice. Alternatively, use the example story as it is, as it will have relevance to most areas of work.

Procedure

1   Ask the students what disasters and accidents can happen at their place of work—not just accidents that cause injuries, but things like break-ins, computers crashing, burst water pipes, etc. List them on the board.

2   In pairs, get the students to imagine that these disasters have happened in their place of study or work, and to complete the relevant parts of a fictional accident report book, with the following headings (which you can write on the board, or copy for them):

Date	Time	Event	Who reported	Witness	Explanation	Action taken

Photocopiable © Oxford University Press

3   Write headline, 'Company to go out of business as result of fire' on the board. Get students to predict what went wrong and what the consequences might be. Then give out the text and get students to identify all the things that the company did wrong.

4   If you want to do some grammar work at this point, you can focus on *should have/shouldn't have* sentences (*They shouldn't have kept so much paper next to an electric fire.*), and third conditionals (*If the management had checked the electrical wiring, it wouldn't have happened.*).

Company to go out of business as result of fire

IT SEEMS THAT faulty electrics and poor staff training were to blame for the fire that destroyed part of an office block in the centre of town last week. Fortunately no one was hurt in the blaze that started in the middle of the afternoon, but Lewis Employment Services, who rent most of the offices in the block, is likely to go out of business because they have lost all their equipment and records.

Chris Lewis, Managing Director of Lewis Employment Services, said, 'Although we are obviously relieved that no one was hurt, this is still a complete disaster for us. We have lost all our computer equipment, all our computer data, and all our records and files. I realise now we should have kept proper computer back-ups and stored records off-site, However, that isn't much comfort at the moment. Because of this fire, we will probably have to close business altogether.'

In spite of the disaster the 34 employees of LES have not lost their jobs. A partner organization of LES has already found work for most of them and expects to find work for the others shortly.

The cause of the fire may have been due to a number of poor procedures on the part of LES. One employee, who didn't want to be named, said that the electrics had been faulty for some time with lights flickering and frequent losses of power. 'If the management had checked the electrical wiring, then this wouldn't have happened.'

The fire is thought to have started in a store cupboard where lots of paper records were kept. Our witness said, 'We shouldn't have kept so much paper near to an electric fire.' Fire extinguishers near the cupboard were apparently not working properly and staff did not know how to use them, despite a recent campaign by local government to improve staff training in emergencies. If the fire services hadn't arrived so quickly, it might have been a lot worse.

Photocopiable © Oxford University Press

5 In pairs, get the students to role-play the interview between the company representative and the Health and Safety Officer investigating the accident. The HSO should take detailed notes.

6 Get the students to choose one of the accidents from their reports in step 2, and write some more details of what the company did wrong in the 'Explanation' column.

7 Get the students to role-play the interview between the HSO and the company, reversing the roles taken in step 5.

Variation

For a shorter activity—and for elementary students—you can leave out the text and role-play steps, and just use the completed accident reports with students interviewing each other about the incidents. This can also avoid the third conditional, which may be a little difficult for elementary students.

Follow-up

Students choose one of the accidents from the table and write a report.

7.7 Spot the danger—risk assessment

Level	Pre-intermediate to advanced
Time	30–40 minutes (plus 30 minutes for step 5)
Aims	LANGUAGE Phrasal verbs; risk language.
	OTHER To raise awareness of health and safety issues through a look at hazards and risk assessment.
Sample topic	Retail and sales
Transfer	Activity can be transferred to any specialism where there is equipment which is used by a number of people. Use a different dangerous workplace picture, as appropriate.
Materials	Picture of a dangerous workplace; 'Risk assessment form' (Worksheet 7.7).

Preparation

Set up the classroom with a few hazards—for example, cable from tape player in a place where people can trip, precarious pile of books on top of cupboard, a broken chair (or anything else you can lay your hands on—but nothing that will seriously cause injury!). Remember to remove the hazard after the discussion in step 1.

Procedure

1 Get students to look around the classroom and identify the hazards you have pre-set. Ask them: *what is the danger? Who is at risk? What can be done to prevent the danger? Are there any other potential dangers in the classroom?*

2 Show the students the picture of a dangerous workplace for two minutes. Hide the picture and get them to write down as many of the dangers as they can remember.

3 Compare answers, and look at the picture again.

4 Complete the 'Risk assessment form' for the dangers in the shop-floor picture. Provide necessary language (for example, *There's a danger of … Someone could …*). You may want to provide the students with a selection of verbs and phrasal verbs (for example, *trip over, fall off, put away, fold up, throw away*).

Worksheet 7.7
Risk assessment form

Hazard (What is the danger?)	At risk (Who is at risk?)	Controls/safe method (What can be done?)
Electric cable across doorway	All staff and members of the public entering the room	Ensure cable goes under carpet, or is run and fixed above door. If needed for temporary work only, either close off door or display hazard sign.

5 Divide the class into groups. Each group should be given a different part of their learning environment:

Example
- corridors and communal areas
- staff room
- café/canteen/kitchen
- toilets and washroom
- storage facilities
- the street outside.

(The exact areas will depend on your teaching situation.)
Send the teams off to carry out a risk assessment, using the form above. Remember that they may not see examples of *actual* dangers: risk assessment looks for *potential* dangers. If the students can't actually be sent out, then get them to think about the areas listed.

6 Get students to think about their own work environment (if appropriate) and to carry out a risk assessment for homework.

Variation 1

Convert the picture into a 'Spot the difference' by copying and making small alterations.

Variation 2

If students are pre-work or do not have much experience of the workplace of their specialism, get them to think about their home environment for step 6.

Follow-up

Write a report on workplace risks with recommendations for how risks can be reduced.

7.8 The dangerous workplace game

Level	Intermediate to advanced
Time	30–40 minutes
Aims	To practise language of dealing with hazards and dangers; to develop fluency skills.
Sample topic	Mechanical trades
Transfer	Activity can be transferred to any specialism, but it will be most effective in places where there are a number of physical and material hazards—Catering, Construction and building trades, Engineering, Horticulture and agriculture, Medicine and health care.
Materials	Cards to make the 'board' of game squares—approx 24 cards per group; a picture of a 'safe' place in the students' workspace—for example, their desk—one per group; dice.

Preparation

Prepare 16 'hazard cards' and approximately eight blank cards. You will need one set for every 4–6 students. (If you have sufficient space, you can make the cards big enough to stand on—so the students can do the journey more physically.)
Suggestions for what to put on the cards for Motor trades, Catering, Construction are given as well as a set of general hazards.

Procedure

1 Ask students if they have heard of Indiana Jones. *What type of problems and hazards does he have to overcome?*

2 Tell the students they are going to play a speaking game based on a similar route through the hazards and dangers found in their workplace.

3 Divide the class into groups of 4–6 students seated around a table. For each group shuffle the cards and place them on the table in a line or connected circle leading to the 'safe' picture.

4 Tell the students that their aim is to get to the 'safe' picture by successfully dealing with the dangers they meet on the way. The students take turns to throw the dice. When they land on one of the hazard cards, they have to say how they would deal with the danger and overcome it. If the rest of the players agree that the solution is a good one, then the player stays on that card for the next go; if not, the player must return to the card they were on before. Players cannot repeat solutions that others have made. The winner is the player who reaches 'safe' first, but they must throw the exact number to land on it.

Hazard cards

General (can be used across a range of specialisms)

You get stuck in the lift on the way to work	The lights suddenly go out	The ground starts shaking—it feels like an earthquake
A colleague needs emergency first aid to a broken arm	Violent work colleague wielding a knife comes at you	Smoke and flames coming out of rubbish bin
Rats	Electrical sparks from a fuse box	A loud explosion (what is it?)

Specific (can be adapted to your specialism)

Mechanical trades: Car repair garage	Catering: Kitchen	Construction: Building site
Pool of motor oil on floor	Pool of cooking oil on floor	Pool of water near an electric cable
Car propped up on pile of bricks	Boiling pot about to fall off cooker	Bucket of paint falling off ladder

Mechanical trades	Catering	Construction
You fall into the car pit and sprain an ankle	You fall down the stairs and sprain an ankle	You fall into a hole and sprain your ankle
A stack of badly piled tyres are falling towards you	Several bags of potatoes have split and are rolling towards you	A pile of bricks is tumbling out of a tipper truck towards you
Chains holding an engine swinging uncontrollably	Meat carcases swinging uncontrollably	Demolition ball and chain swinging uncontrollably
Water starts flooding through the workshop	Water starts flooding through the kitchen	Water starts flooding through the building site

Variation 1

The precise way you play the game can be adapted to fit the space and furniture where you are teaching (and also if your students have an aversion to 'playing games'). You can avoid the dice throwing and board altogether, by simply having the students draw a card in turn from the top of a pile of hazard cards.

Variation 2

With more motivated and experienced students you can get them to think of some of the hazards to put on the cards.

Variation 3

To make the game last longer, you can either add more cards (hazard, blank, or alternative situations), or use a coin instead of a dice—students toss the coin and move one space for heads, two for tails.

7.9 Disability awareness

Level Intermediate to advanced

Time 30–40 minutes

Aims LANGUAGE Discussing possibility, modals, conditionals.

OTHER To look at the practicalities of adapting one's workplace to people with disability; to understand the work situation from the perspective of a disabled person.

Sample topic General

Materials Blank cards or pieces of paper—20 pieces per group.

Disability is a sensitive area, but that does not mean that it should be avoided. You will need to think carefully about how best to approach it. If you have disabled students in the class, you should talk to them first on their own and ask how they feel about discussing this area and if they want to take a lead role in it. Even if you do not have students with disabilities, the issue still needs to be treated with seriousness and maturity—and you should probably tell the class well before that you are planning such a lesson (so that people, who you may not be aware of having a connection with disability, can express their feelings about it).

Preparation

None, unless you feel the students will not be able to come up with ideas for the cards in steps 1 and 2—in which case prepare these in advance.

Procedure

1 Ask students if any of their work colleagues or friends and family are disabled. Build up a list of types of disability—mobility (wheelchair user, limb incapacity), vision or hearing impairment, conditions such as heart disease and asthma, psychological and mental disability. You may want to include other temporary conditions such as a sprained wrist, pregnancy.

2 Give out about twenty cards (or pieces of paper) to groups of three or four students. On half of them ask them to write a disability (they can repeat if necessary). On the other half they should write a job (for example, *police officer, teacher, mechanic*) or a place (*stairs, computer workstation, building site, ladder*). The jobs and places should be general at this step, and not related to their specialism.

3 Collect in the separate piles of cards and redistribute them to the groups. The groups turn over a card from the top of each pile and discuss the implications—for example, *wheelchair-user* and *computer workstation*, or *hearing impairment* and *police officer*. The students should discuss how the two can be compatible, what changes and adaptations will be necessary, and—if nothing else is possible—what nearest alternatives can be found. Do not let the students give up too soon on finding a solution.

4 Report back for whole-class discussion.

5 Now get the students to think about their own specialism and their own workplaces. How can they be adapted? You could get them to produce actual designs to help certain disabilities. Alternatively, they can imagine that they are taking a disabled person on a tour of their workplace (or the school if they are pre-work)—*How do they have to modify the standard tour?*

Variation

You could ask students, particularly pre-work, to think about how they would adapt their own home for disability access.

Follow-up

Get students to find out about disability laws in their country and how they affect their place of work or study.

8
Evaluation and review

Evaluation and review is an important part of the world of work—
evaluating job performance, setting targets, appraisal interviews,
quality testing (of products and services), as well as the attainment of
specific qualifications, feature in some form or other in all
specialisms. In-work learners will already be aware of this and pre-
work learners will need to be ready for a world of evaluation and
review that will go beyond the educational testing that they are
familiar with.

Testing, whether it be learner assessment or course evaluation, is a
central and integrated component of ESP teaching. An ESP course
will almost certainly have very specific objectives, aiming to equip
particular learners to do particular things, and formal testing will
occur in the form of *placement* tests (what are the needs and potential
of the learners and which course should they be placed in?),
achievement tests (is the learner keeping up with the course and have
they absorbed what has been taught?), and *proficiency* tests (can the
learner perform certain language tasks and function in certain
situations?).

Depending on the institution and the teaching situation you are in,
such tests may be given to you to administer with little input from
yourself, or you may have to produce them yourself. Whichever, it is
important to see evaluation, review, and testing as part of an ongoing
process throughout the course. All students, and perhaps especially
ESP students, will need to see what they have achieved and the
progress they have made, and its importance beyond the classroom—
the *value* in evaluation, if you like. At the same time, they will need to
know where they still have to get to.

It is important to go beyond formal testing. In ESP such testing is
only part of the wider context of evaluation and review. A culture of
evaluation, self-assessment and self-awareness should pervade the
course. In other words, learners should not only become aware of
what they lack—their needs and the ability to assess how they are
working towards meeting them—but also their strengths and
potential and how they are developing and harnessing these.
Evaluation and review should be a positive feature: not just
identifying gaps and needs, but also drawing attention to strengths
and areas worthy of praise. 8.1, 'Give yourself a star' to 8.3, 'Car boot
sale' focus on this aspect, while 8.4, 'Design a test' to 8.6, 'Ten
question test' look at more formal testing procedures.

Evaluation and review does not only apply to learners. The course itself and your own performance as teacher should also be evaluated and reviewed using formal feedback procedures (for example, questionnaires) and informal discussions (*How do you think it's going?*), as well as asking yourself questions and assessing how well you are meeting your own objectives. The final activity 8.7, 'How did you do?' is designed to help with this.

8.1 Give yourself a star

Level Elementary to advanced

Time 20–30 minutes

Aims LANGUAGE Simple past; present perfect.

OTHER To review recent achievements; to raise self-awareness and a sense of pride.

Sample topic General

Transfer Activity can be used in any specialism where reviewing work and identifying success is important, but is especially relevant to those which require the completion of regular work records and reports.

Procedure

1 Write two columns on the board: *work/study* and *social/leisure*. Tell the class about two or three of your personal achievements for the past week. For example, *marked half-term assignments, taught a good class on report-writing, went for a run, visited an old friend I hadn't seen for ages.*

2 Get the students to think of ten things they've achieved (and feel pleased with) in the last week, dividing them into the two columns. You can work on the grammar of present perfect (*I've written three reports this week*) and simple past tenses (*I dealt with a difficult customer very effectively on Monday*) at this point if you want, by introducing specific time references. Make sure that in the 'work/study' column, students focus on achievements and outcomes that can transfer into any work records or reports that they need to complete in their specialism.

3 Get the students to choose one achievement from each column which they are most proud of and award it a 'gold star'.

4 In pairs, students ask and tell each other about their 'gold star' achievements.

5 In groups, extend the period of review backwards for a full year and think of five achievements in each of the two categories. For each student the group should decide what they think are the best achievements and award Gold, Silver, and Bronze medals.

Variation

For students with little experience of their specialism, the first column can focus either on a work placement or a holiday/part-time job, or on their English language studies rather than work.

Follow-up

Carry out the activity at regular intervals to build up a record of achievement.

8.2 Appraisal and targets

Level Pre-intermediate to advanced

Time 40–50 minutes

Aims LANGUAGE Present perfect simple and continuous; future intentions and plans (*I'm going to …* vs *Maybe I'll …*).

OTHER To review past achievements; to set targets for future achievements and discuss ways of reaching them.

Sample topic General

Transfer Activity can be used with any specialism, but will be most useful in specialisms where there is a clear developmental career path.

Materials Pieces of paper; photocopies of Worksheet 8.2 (for Variation)—one per student.

Procedure

1 Choose a famous person that the class will recognize—for example, the President/Prime Minister or a football star. In class, carry out an 'appraisal' by thinking of three achievements and three disappointments that the person has had in the last year.

2 Use the context of the famous person to practise the language of discussing recent achievements and activities (present perfect simple and continuous).

Example He's been playing really well this season, but he hasn't scored many goals.

3 Ask students to write down three achievements from the last year in their work or studies, and three negative points (for example, something that didn't go as they planned, something where they felt 'out of their depth', or a mistake they made). Tell them that the information is confidential and will not be shared, so they should be honest with themselves in this 'self-appraisal' step.

4 Give out the blank pieces of paper (about four or five per student) and ask them to write a 'target' on each. For example, it could be a qualification they want to get or a professional (or personal) relationship they want to improve. Encourage the use of *going to* for definite plans or *I'd like to/maybe I'll* for less definite ideas.

Example I'm going to learn a third language. Maybe I'll use it to get a better position.

5 Collect in the pieces of paper (which should be anonymous) and redistribute them to groups of 3-4 students.

6 Get the groups to consider each target in turn and plan a course of action to help achieve it, which they should write on the original pieces of paper. Pin the pieces of paper on a board or wall for later (anonymous) collection.

7 Return to the famous personality from step 1. Get the class to set targets and ways of achieving them for him/her.

8 Finish the class by getting the students to collect their targets to find out what course of action the others have set for them.

Variation

Instead of step 3 above, get students to complete an actual appraisal form, either on their own or in a role-play situation. Here is an example form to use:

Worksheet 8.2

Appraisal form

Name: _____

Job title: _____

Changes in duties/responsibilities in last year: _____

_____

Achievements in last year: _____

_____

Main strengths: _____

_____

Main weaknesses: _____

_____

Training and development needs: _____

_____

Relations with managers: _____

Relations with colleagues: _____

Action plan: _____

_____

Other information: _____

_____

Photocopiable © Oxford University Press

Follow-up

If you want to give further practice of the language of future intentions (*going to,* etc.), then you can add a further step whereby students write out what they are going to do on the basis of the plans of action that have been set. This could be done for homework.

Comments

Some elements of the activity as described might be too intrusive or personal for your teaching situation. If this is the case, then keep the whole activity in the area of famous people, giving out roles if necessary. Students can do parallel activities for themselves as homework or private study.

8.3 Car boot sale

Level Pre-intermediate to advanced

Time 40–50 minutes

Aims LANGUAGE A range of functional language.

OTHER To set targets and work towards achieving them, accepting compromise; to evaluate a task.

Sample topic General

Transfer Activity is of special relevance to Marketing and advertising, and Retail and sales.

Preparation

If you want the students to bring in actual items, you will need to explain this in a previous session.

Procedure

1 Explain what a 'car boot sale' is (sometimes called a 'garage sale'): people sell items that they no longer need and which they display in an informal marketplace.

2 Ask the students to think of five items they want to get rid of, either from home or work. (If possible they can bring the actual items in.) They write them down and give each one of them two prices: the price they would like to get for the item, and the lowest price they would accept. Their target is to sell all five items for the maximum price.

3 The students get up and mingle, trying to sell their items to each other. They have to accept that they may not get their 'asking price'. They may also want to buy something in exchange. Encourage students to bargain and haggle. They must also record any deals they make. You may want to input/revise the functional language of explanation, persuasion, and negotiation before this step:

Example Explaining what something is—*It's used for –ing, It's made of …*
Persuading someone to buy something —*You'll find it really useful. It'll make your life much more … You really ought to think about …*
Negotiation—*How about if I come down on the price a bit? What would you like to offer? I'm not sure it's worth that much.*

4 Set a time limit—15 or 20 minutes—and give regular time warnings.

5   At the end of the time limit, get the students to sit back and in pairs review how successful they were, both in terms of income against expenditure and the number of their original items they sold. Who was the most successful?

6   As a group, evaluate the task. What went well? What went badly? How could they have been more successful?

Variation 1

If you think the students will have trouble thinking of five items, you can give them pictures from a magazine or catalogue. But the activity will be better if they use their own items.

Variation 2

Define the items they can sell more precisely—for example, only items relevant to the specialism. Or you can include some 'abstract' items, such as skills that they no longer need—or even experiences that they've had.

Follow-up

Produce a balance sheet of transactions (mainly for students in Finance and accounts-based specialisms).

8.4 Design a test

Level   Intermediate to advanced

Time   40–50 minutes

Aims   LANGUAGE Present simple passive.

OTHER   To introduce the concept of quality tests; to design a quality test relevant to the specialism.

Sample topic   General

Transfer   Activity can be used with any manufacturing or product-based specialism where technical equipment is used. For students working in service-based areas, you can use procedures and systems instead.

Materials   Everyday items (optional)—for example, laptop computer, mobile phone, work bag

Procedure

1   Get students to brainstorm all the different tests they have done in their lives, not just academic and professional tests (for example, school exams, entrance exams, vocational/professional qualifications), but others like medical tests (eye tests, blood tests), and driving/cycling tests. They can also include things like 'tests of strength' at the fair, and magazine-style personality tests.

Encourage personalization at this step: *Are you good at tests? Which type of tests are you best/worst at?*

2 Ask students what type of tests are used in their specialism. Lead them to the idea of *quality* tests, which are used in some form or another in most specialisms.

3 Choose two everyday items, such as a car and a sofa (or, if you are using real objects, a laptop computer or mobile phone, etc.). Ask the students what the important qualities of each are.

Example Car: *safety, speed, comfort, environmentally-friendly*
Sofa: *comfort, 'cleanability', safety (i.e. fire-proof)*

4 Discuss in whole class, how these qualities are tested, especially the safety ones. Complete a chart like Worksheet 8.4, giving them the first line as an example. Elicit ideas for the three other qualities from the students.

Worksheet 8.4
Product: Car

Quality	Test	Comment
Safety	A car is driven at various speeds into a solid wall. The impact zone and the effect on the dummy passengers is measured.	Requires specialist facilities and equipment.
Speed		
Comfort		
Environmentally friendly		

Photocopiable © Oxford University Press

5 Divide the students into pairs or small groups. Get them to think of (or give them) other everyday items, this time ones that you do not necessarily associate with quality tests. For example: a pencil or a coffee mug, etc.

6 In pairs, get students to decide the qualities that are needed for their items and to design tests to check and measure the quality. They can use Worksheet 8.4 as a guide.

7 Get the students to describe to the whole class the quality tests they have come up with. As the theme of the activity is quality testing, you should take the opportunity to emphasize your own role as a quality tester and do some overt correction of language, especially the use of the present simple passive.

Variation

Substitute the everyday items suggested in step 3 with real items from the students' specialism—for example, for phone-based services you could use ear-pieces, microphones, layout of data screens, etc.

Follow-up

Transfer the same approach to products and equipment from the specialism, and discuss the equipment and systems that are used to test quality and how effective they are. For example, in information technology or engineering you might look at the various pieces of equipment which are used to test electronic circuits—multimeter, oscilloscope, logic probe, function generator.

8.5 Theory and practice tests

Level Pre-intermediate to advanced

Time 50–60 minutes

Aims LANGUAGE Question forms.

OTHER To look in detail at a proficiency test (driving) and transfer the same approach to designing a proficiency test for the specialism.

Sample topic Tourism and travel; Construction and building trades

Transfer Activity can be transferred to any specialism where there can be both a theory and a practical element to testing.

Materials Realia to simulate the practical areas of specialism; 'Theory test' questions for the specialism (see examples below).

Preparation

Be ready to set up realia for the practical test of the specialism you are going to test. For example, for a tour guide, furniture arranged as a coach, and a microphone; for the painter and decorator, ladders, brushes and possibly paint.

Procedure

1 Find out who can drive and who passed their driving test most recently. Discuss what happened in the test—*where did it take place? What components were there? Was there a theory and a practical test?* If the students did not take a theory and a practical test, then explain that many driving tests consist of a test on the theory of driving and road safety, and a practical test on the road of driving skills. Discuss and compare the different manoeuvres that are tested (three-point turn, emergency stop, etc.).

2 Get a willing student to be tested for start procedures when driving—i.e. they mime getting into an imaginary car, putting on seat-belt, adjusting mirror, starting engine, checking mirror, indicating, etc. This is to establish the idea of a practical element in the test they are going to prepare for their specialism.

3　In groups, get students to think about their own specialism. What are the equivalent 'theory' and 'practical' elements? For example, what 'manoeuvres' will you want to test?

4　In groups, students write some questions for the theory test (or you can supply your own—for example, from a training manual). They can be direct questions, multiple-choice, or *true/false*.

Example

Questions for tour guide

True or false?

- When giving a guided tour on a coach you should always face the direction you are travelling.
  (*False—you should try to face the passengers at least some of the time, …, if it is safe to do so*).

- When giving a guided tour on a coach you should always introduce your driver to the passengers.
  (*True*)

- The day before a guided coach tour you should phone the coach company to check that everything is arranged—meeting time and place, itinerary, microphone, etc.
  (*True*)

- It is acceptable to ask for tips at the end of a tour.
  (*Depends on the culture*)

Written questions:

- Give the dates when three famous buildings in your city were built.

- If you are stuck in traffic on a coach tour, what three general subjects can you talk about?

Questions for painter and decorator

- What type of paint is best for the following surfaces: plaster walls, interior woodwork, exterior woodwork, radiators, stone work?
  (*Answers, respectively: emulsion, undercoat and gloss, undercoat and weather-proof gloss, metal paint, masonry paint*)

- What safety equipment is needed when working at heights?
  (*Answer: scaffold tower and boards, and possibly a safety harness*)

- How many litres of paint will be needed to cover the interior walls of a building with 23 rooms each with a wall surface of 64 sq metres?
  (*Answer: approximately 120 litres, assuming coverage of 12–15 square metres per litre*)

8.6 Ten question test

Level Elementary to advanced

Time 10 minutes set-up for Session 1, 30–40 minutes for Session 2

Aims To revise language and subject areas covered in the course; to involve students in the production of a quick test.

Sample topic General

Procedure

The activity takes place over two separate days, as students will need time to prepare.

Session 1

1 Tell students that they are going to have a test in the next class, but that they are going to write the questions.

2 Ask students to look back at the whole course (or whatever area you want to cover). They can revise in any way they want, but they must also prepare ten questions—five related to English language, and five more specifically to the subject (including vocabulary as well as subject knowledge). Tell them that the questions should be comprehensive, but also easy to mark. They should also know the answers to the questions they are setting.

Session 2

1 Put the students in pairs. Ask them to look at each other's questions and to decide on the best ten for a test. They should cover the full range and be at different levels of difficulty.

2 Each pair takes turns to come to the front of the class and be the Quizmasters for the rest of the students, who should write down their answers.

3 At the end of each set of ten questions, the Quizmasters should go through the answers. Students can self-mark.

4 After every pair has administered their tests, decide who was the winner—both in terms of getting the most correct answers, but also in setting the best test.

Variation 1

Do the test as a quiz. Pairs of students go round and visit other pairs and take turns to be quizmasters and contestants. Contestants give the answer or say 'pass'. Quizmasters say 'correct' or give the correct answers (and go through 'passes' at the end).

Variation 2

In larger classes, students can work in smaller groups or write fewer questions.

Follow-up

Students revise the answers they got wrong.

5 When they have prepared five or six theory questions, get the groups to decide the practical criteria they want to test. Obviously, the effectiveness of these criteria will depend on how closely you can simulate the practical test conditions.

Example

Practical criteria for tour guide

- Friendliness (for example, when passengers are boarding th coach)
- Clear voice
- Interesting and entertaining information
- Good eye contact
- Clear instructions (for example, for meeting time)

Practical criteria for painter and decorator

- Use of appropriate brushes
- Correct and safe use of ladders and other support eq
- Regular and even brushwork
- Neat brushwork around windows and other featur example, light switches)
- Use of appropriate materials for cleaning brushes

6 Get the groups to take turns to administer their tests, and theory, on the rest of the class.

7 Assess both the people doing the test (did they pass quality of the test (was it a good test?).

Variation 1

Omit either the theory or practical test, if you fee appropriate for your specialism. Alternatively, g class to design the theory test, and the other ha practical.

Variation 2

Carry out the activity as described above, but administering the test to each other, get the administer the test to you—in other words the spot! Students who are not normally m element of role-reversal.

Follow-up

You can refine the tests in the light of th administering them, and write them u the future.

Comments

You can use the whole activity as a diagnostic activity for you to assess areas of difficulty in the class, both in terms of language and content, and thus set an appropriate formal test in a later class.

8.7 How did *you* do?

This is not a classroom activity like the others, but really just for the teacher's own benefit and self-improvement. However, if you are brave, you can involve the students, as suggested in 'Procedure' below.

Time 15 minutes for step 1, 15 minutes for step 4, if you decide to involve the students.

Aims To evaluate your own performance as a teacher, and to set goals and targets for improving.

Materials Photocopies of Course feedback form—one per student.

Preparation

Photocopy the Course feedback form, or write your own.

Procedure

1 Ask the students to complete a course feedback form. This could be the one that the institution where you are working provides, or a very simple design.

 a A list of the syllabus and classes for the course with columns to grade different aspects, such as 'General', 'Materials', 'Usefulness', and 'Teaching'.

 b A chart with headings for 'Things I liked', 'Things I didn't like'— and why. The form can cover a range of areas including, for example, administration, facilities and equipment, classroom activities, application to specialism, quality of teaching.

 c A form that focuses on the content of lessons. There is an example opposite.

2 Take the feedback forms away and analyze them with particular reference to your own performance in the class. Are there things you could have done better or differently in the areas that got low grades? What made the areas that got good grades successful?

3 Complete a self-feedback form, with headings such as:
 • Things I did well
 • Things I didn't do well
 • Techniques and methodological areas (for example, writing, role-play, warmers, tests) I need to do more/less of
 • Subject areas, language skills, and job skills related to the specialism that I need to work on
 • Further areas where I could develop
 • Things I could pass onto other teachers working with similar groups

Course feedback form

What changes would you like in your lessons?	Changes (please circle)			Other comments
Speaking	No change	More	Less	
Listening	No change	More	Less	
Reading	No change	More	Less	
Writing	No change	More	Less	
Grammar	No change	More	Less	
Pronunciation	No change	More	Less	
Error Correction	No change	More	Less	
Vocabulary	No change	More	Less	
Progress Tests	No change	More	Less	
Use of Coursebook	No change	More	Less	
Homework	No change	More	Less	
Pairwork	No change	More	Less	
Class Games	No change	More	Less	
Use of Video	No change	More	Less	
Songs	No change	More	Less	
Computer Programmes	No change	More	Less	
Internet	No change	More	Less	

- You can also give yourself an overall grade. The important thing is to be honest—honest about your strengths and successes as well as your weaknesses.

4 Optional final step: if you have the right sort of class (and only you will know if you do), share your self-feedback with the students and ask for their honest opinion.

Variation

Do the feedback activity in conjunction with a colleague—especially a colleague who has been involved with the same course. You can either do steps 2 and 3 with your colleague, or just step 4.

Index

References are to page numbers first, then activity numbers